SENSATIONAL WAYS TO DECORATE PAPER,

STAMPING
WITH STYLE

FABRIC, POLYMER CLAY & MORE

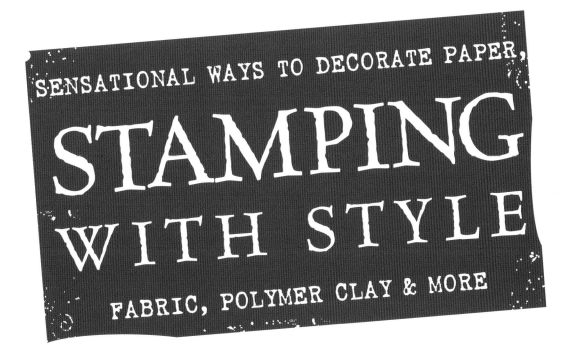

SENSATIONAL WAYS TO DECORATE PAPER,

STAMPING
WITH STYLE

FABRIC, POLYMER CLAY & MORE

Katherine Duncan Aimone

LARK BOOKS

A Division of Sterling Publishing Company, Inc.

NEW YORK

This book is dedicated to
STEVE AIMONE,
my patient and loving partner.

Many thanks to
ART SNYDER
of Rubberstampmadness for his
support and infusion of expertise
during the process if writing
this book.

Art Director:
Susan McBride

Photo Stylist:
Chris Bryant

Photographer:
Evan Bracken

Illustrator:
Orrin Lundgren

Production Assistant:
Hannes Charen

Editorial Assistance:
Veronika Alice Gunter,
Rain Newcomb

Library of Congress Cataloging-in-Publication Data

Duncan-Aimone, Katherine
    Stamping with style : sensational ways to decorate paper, fabric, polymer clay, and more / by Katherine Duncan-Aimone
    p. cm.
Includes index.
ISBN 1-57990-133-6 (hardcover) 1-57990-380-0 (paperback)
  1. Rubber stamp printing. 2. Interior decoration--Amateurs' manual. I. Title

TT867 .D86 2001
761--dc21   2001023523

10 9 8 7 6 5 4 3 2

Published by Lark Books, a division of
Sterling Publishing Co., Inc.
387 Park Avenue South, New York, N.Y. 10016

First Paperback Edition 2002
© 2001, Lark Books

Distributed in Canada by Sterling Publishing,
c/o Canadian Manda Group, One Atlantic Ave., Suite 105
Toronto, Ontario, Canada M6K 3E7

Distributed in the U.K. by:
Guild of Master Craftsman Publications Ltd.
Castle Place, 166 High Street, Lewes East Sussex, England BN7 1XU
Tel: (+ 44) 1273 477374, Fax: (+ 44) 1273 478606,
Email: pubs@thegmcgroup.com, Web: www.gmcpublications.com

Distributed in Australia by Capricorn Link (Australia) Pty Ltd., P.O. Box 704, Windsor, NSW 2756 Australia

The written instructions, photographs, designs, patterns, and projects in this volume are intended for the personal use of the reader and may be reproduced for that purpose only. Any other use, especially commercial use, is forbidden under law without written permission of the copyright holder.

Every effort has been made to ensure that all the information in this book is accurate. However, due to differing conditions, tools, and individual skills, the publisher cannot be responsible for any injuries, losses, and other damages that may result from the use of the information in this book.

If you have questions or comments about this book, please contact:
Lark Books
67 Broadway
Asheville, NC 28801
(828) 236-9730

Printed in China

ISBN 1-57990-133-6 (hardcover) 1-57990-380-0 (paperback)

Table of Contents

Introduction

"The joy you feel the first time you plop an image on paper with a stamp is so intense that you never want to give it up! You want more! Since people have such small amounts of free time to spend creatively, stamping is a perfect fit for today. You can stamp anywhere, and you can stamp for a few minutes or all day. It allows your own personality to show through. You begin because it's so easy, and stay because it's so satisfying. It's wonderful to see stamping progressing as an art form because people stay with this hobby for the long haul."

—MaryJo McGraw, stamp artist, teacher, and author

Stamping is an extremely popular mode of artistic expression for both artists and crafters. Even if you haven't tried stamping yourself, you're bound to have read about it or seen examples of it. There are so many ways to use this medium creatively, that artists and crafters keep discovering more and more applications for stamping. And the well is far from dry!

Stamps abound everywhere. From home supply to art and craft stores, you'll find a variety of ready-made stamps to fit any idea that you have. If you want to make your own stamps, you can carve them with some basic tools, convert everyday objects into stamps, or use natural materials such as leaves to create sophisticated designs. Stamping can also be done without transferring ink to a surface—you can use alternative techniques such as stamping fabric with bleach, heat stamping velvet, and imprinting polymer clay.

This book of 40 elegant projects will introduce you to the newest wave of stamping with its seemingly unlimited choices. From home decor to wearables, the wonderful projects were created by some of the top designers in the field. Through step-by-step instructions you'll learn how to use everything from rubber stamps to shoe treads to create interesting surfaces. Whether you transform a junk CD into a sophisticated clock, dress up plain wrapping paper, or make stamped polymer clay jewelry, you'll probably find that stamping has more applications than you imagined.

So clear off your dining room table, pick out a project that grabs you, gather your materials, and get to know one of the most versatile mediums on the market today!

CD Clocks by Lynn B. Krucke show an inventive way to use stamping to dress up an old CD.

Basic Materials and Techniques

Whether you choose to transfer an image to a surface with a simple carved potato or a ready-made rubber stamp, you'll soon discover the marvelous possibilities of stamping. If you're new to the world of stamping, the following section will bring you up to speed on everything you need to know to begin.

Simple stamps can be made from a variety of materials, such as vegetables, fruits, leaves, and household materials. You can also purchase an unlimited variety of ready-made rubber stamps from craft and stamp stores. Foam stamps are a great choice for stamping fabric or large surfaces.

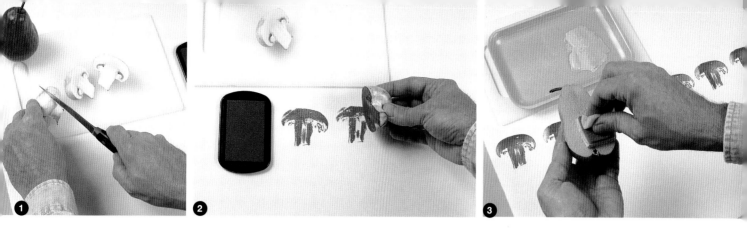

Stamping with Everyday Things

The simplest of stamps can be made with items that can be found in your home and yard. Fruits and vegetables have inherent shapes that make them a natural for printing. Try this exercise to get started: Slice a vegetable, such as a mushroom, in half (photo 1) and dab it with a paper towel to remove excess moisture. You've now produced a simple stamp that you can ink and print (photo 2). The unpredictable results of printing with a natural surface is part of the charm of this type of stamping. Slice a piece of fruit, such as a pear, in half and apply ink or paint to this larger surface

with a foam applicator (photo 3). Print this image, and you'll begin to create an interesting design (photo 4). You can embellish stamped designs such as these with simple drawn lines (photo 5).

Another simple exercise that will produce instant, and often stunning, results is printing with fresh leaves. Collect leaves that you like from the woods or your yard. Pay attention to the edges of the leaves, and whether they will render interesting shapes when they're printed.

9

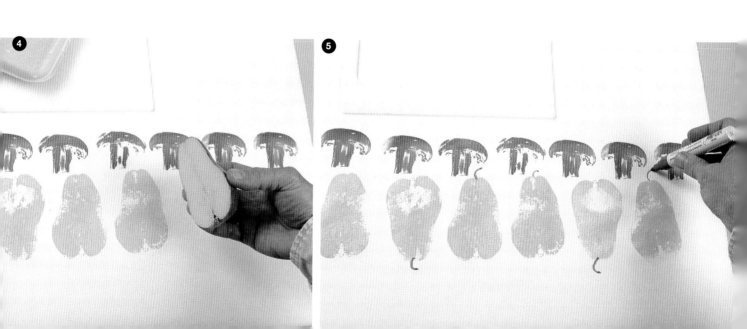

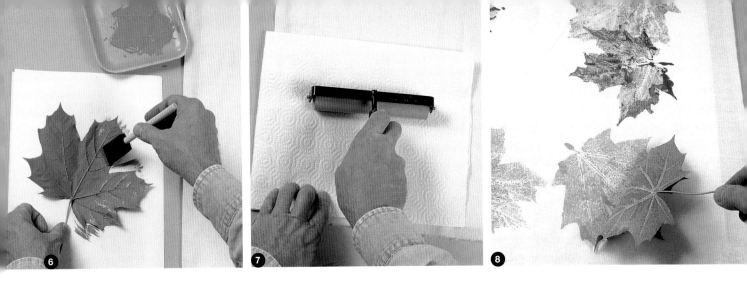

Ink the backside of the leaf (photo 6). (A foam brush works well for this purpose.) Place the inked leaf face-down on your printing surface, cover it with a paper towel to prevent smearing, and press the surface with a rolling pin or printer's brayer (photo 7). Lift each leaf from the surface to reveal an impression of its delicate veins and contours (photo 8). Layer more leaf prints in different colors to suggest the natural scattering of leaves in nature.

Look further, and you'll begin to find more possibilities for stamps. For instance, look in your utensil drawer, and you may find that a functional thing such as a potato masher has interesting lines. Ink the flat end of it with some non-toxic paint or ink, and stamp a design with it.

Our masher produced a delicate, wavy-lined print that you probably wouldn't guess came from an everyday source (photo 9). Add some dots of color with the ends

of wine corks, and you'll begin to see the limitless possibilities of printing with the things in your environment (photo 10).

You might also try printing with old keys, metal hardware such as washers, junk CDs, scraps of wood, pieces of cardboard, uncooked pasta, nut halves, or pieces of carpet padding.

(Note: always use non-toxic paints or inks that you can completely wash away afterwards when printing with anything that you use for food preparation, or, better yet, designate those items for printing only.)

Carving a Simple Stamp

Many of us have had the childhood experience of carving a potato to make a stamp—an exercise which takes the previous one of stamping with halved fruits

10

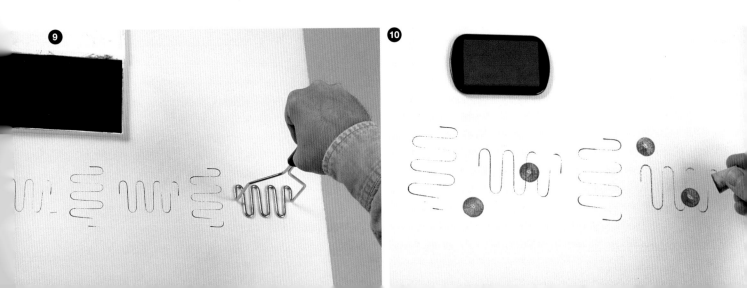

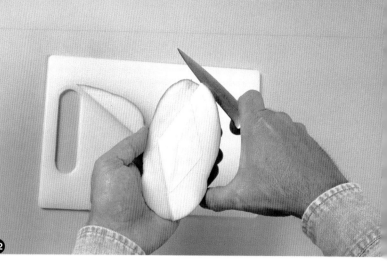

or vegetables a step further. Carving a potato will introduce you to making an original stamp.

To do this, all you'll need are some basic items from your kitchen and paint or an ink pad. Begin by slicing the potato in half. To make carving easy, press a cookie cutter into the sliced half to create a ready-made outline (photo 11). Carve away the excess potato with a paring knife to reveal the shape (photo 12). When you do this, you'll learn something fundamental about how any stamp is made: the printed image of a stamp is created by the raised portion that is left after the other portions of the surface have been carved away.

Carving Stamps from Rubber

Remember making a simple stamp by carving a linoleum block or an eraser when you were a kid? The same process is now used to carve ready-made sheets of soft rubber that are a lot easier to carve than their improvised predecessors. These sheets are safe for children to use with supervision.

You can purchase these inexpensive sheets of rubber at craft or art supply stores. You'll also need transfer paper, a pencil, and a permanent black marker for copying your image to the sheet; and a set of linoleum carving tools and a craft knife for carving. For printing the stamp in the traditional manner of printmakers, you'll need a sheet of glass, a large glazed ceramic tile, a disposable food tray, or other water repellent surface to use as a palette, as well as a brayer and ink or paint. You can also print your stamp with ink from a stamp pad.

Inexpensive sheets of rubber made for carving are available at art and craft supply stores. Add a simple-to-use set of linoleum carving tools, and you'll be ready to carve your own stamps.

11

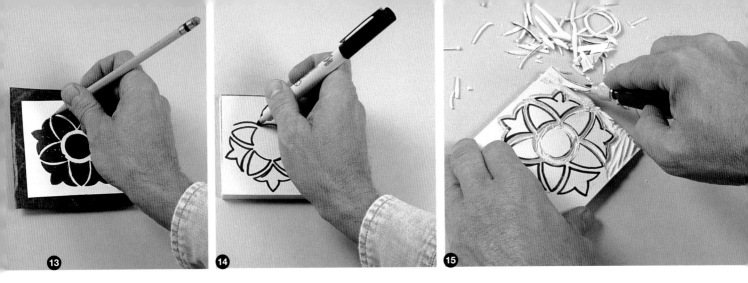

Carving can be a cinch if you take it one step at a time. First, draw or trace a simple image or design of your choice on a sheet of paper, keeping in mind that the design will be reversed when you print it. Outline the basic shape of the image with your marker. Place a sheet of transfer paper facedown on the rubber sheet (or block), and trace the lines of your image with a pencil (photo 13). Lift a corner of the transfer paper to make sure that the image has been sufficiently copied to the sheet. Redraw lines as necessary.

Remove the transfer paper, and use the permanent black marker to trace the lines of your image on the sheet, making them easier to see (photo 14). As you look at the lines, remember that you'll be carving away the areas that you want to disappear from the image, and leaving the areas raised that you want to print. Begin by outlining the shape with one of the smaller-tipped carving tools. Always point the blade away from yourself, and hold it at a slight angle to the sur-

face of the carving sheet while you shave off a thin layer of the sheet. Don't attempt to gouge the rubber — use smooth, easy, deliberate strokes. Use a broader blade to remove larger excess areas of the sheet as you define the boundaries of your stamp (photo 15).

To ink your stamp with a brayer, first squeeze ink or paint onto your palette (photo 16). Roll the brayer back and forth with smooth, consistent strokes to spread the ink or paint (photo 17). Lift the brayer at the end of each stroke before covering the same ground again. Once the brayer has an even coat on it, roll it on the surface of your carved block (photo 18). Roll the brayer across and off of the block, and repeat from another angle to even out the coverage. Use firm, even pressure to apply the stamp to your printing surface (photo 19).

Voila! You've printed an original, never-seen-before image of your own invention.

12

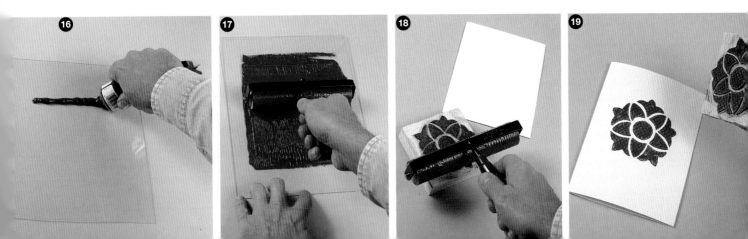

Ready-made Stamps:
So Many Stamps,
So Little Time!

"Rubber stamping allows everyone to be an artist, to experience the joy of creativity that lies within. Age, training, education and experience — they simply don't matter when a person picks up a rubber stamp and discovers its magic. With its potential to work by itself or with other media, from collage to painting and beyond, the rubber stamp literally knows no bounds."

— Art Snyder, Contributing Editor
for *Rubberstampmadness*

Ready-made stamps give you access to a seemingly infinite world of images. It's likely that you have a store in your area that is dedicated to selling stamps and supplies or that your local craft store has dedicated a sizeable area to these products.

Commercial stamps are usually made of rubber or foam mounted on handles. (Stamps are also sold in sheets that can be mounted.) Clubs, magazines, and conferences focus on the subject of rubber stamping, while new techniques and products are constantly being discovered and developed.

A rubber stamp begins with camera-ready art, such as an artist's drawing, a computer-designed drawing, or a photograph. (All art must be copyright-free or approved for rubber stamp usage.) The black-and-white art is etched onto a metal plate through a technical process, and this plate becomes the master plate that is used to create a mold. After the mold is made, bulk rubber is pressed into the molds to make the stamps that are (usually) cut and mounted on wooden handles to make them easier to use.

Rubber stamps precisely replicate drawings (photo 20). These images can be used on a host of materials in ways that are as varied as the imaginations of the crafters who use them. Stamps are often used in combination with other media such as paints, colored pencils or markers, or chalks (photo 21). The images can be repeated to make a pattern, or stamped as a single image in the midst of other elements. They can be layered with paper and other media to create evocative collaged surfaces.

This detail of Kathy Anderson's **Mona Lisa Altar** shows the possibilities of layering papers and stamped images.

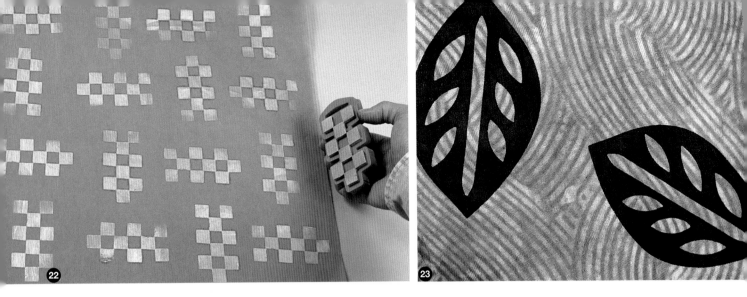

Rubber stamps come in a variety of categories, such as image stamps (representational images), border stamps (motifs that are repeatedly stamped to form a border), alphabet and number stamps (used for adding phrases or simply as design motifs), and pattern stamps (often used to cover a large area that is used as a background for stamping images).

Foam stamps have larger, less delineated designs than rubber stamps, and broad surfaces which produce solid areas of printed color. They are often used to stamp repeated patterns or borders (photo 22). They work well for stamping pieces of fabric because they hold plenty of paint for printing (photo 23). Because of their flexibility, they can be used with success to stamp on curved surfaces.

It's important to clean the surfaces of your stamps after you've used them. Commercial cleaners work especial-ly well for cleaning foam-based stamps (photo 24). Blot the stamp on a paper towel after you've applied the cleaner, and continue until you completely remove the ink (photo 25). You can clean your stamps with mild detergent and water if you're using water-based inks or paints.

Both foam and rubber stamps can be found on mount-ed rollers in home supply and craft stores. These stamps are typically used for adding borders to paint-ed walls, but can be used to roll a continuous pattern onto any printable surface (photo 26).

Inks and Paints

There are lots of inks and paints on the market, and the differences between them often determine the surfaces for which they are recommended. Once you under-stand the basics of why some combinations work and

14

others don't, the choices will become clearer. To make things easier, many manufacturers have developed stamping media for use on a variety of surfaces.

The following section will give you some basic guidelines for choosing a stamping medium. If you're in doubt about the ink or paint that you're about to buy, read the manufacturer's specifications on the product or ask a store clerk for advice. Always try out the coloring medium on the intended surface to see how it behaves before you take on a large project.

It's helpful to know that matching inks or paints to a surface (such as various kinds of paper, fabric, wood, etc.) depends in a large part on how porous the surface is. For instance, water-based pigment inks—commonly used for stamping—have to be absorbed in order to dry thoroughly. For this reason, a surface such as uncoated paper works well with this ink. In contrast, this ink simply won't dry if you use it on coated stock, and you'll end up with a smeary mess on your hands. By contrast, solvent-based inks that dry through evaporation work well on coated paper.

A wide range of stamping media is available, including stamp pads and inks, as well as bottles of ink that can be applied with a printmaker's brayer or a foam-tipped applicator. Use colored markers to add color and dimension to your stamped images.

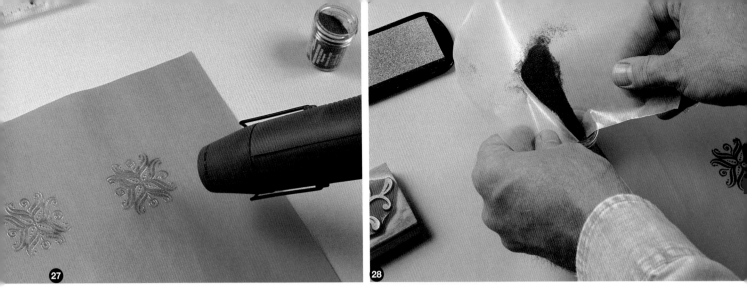

As another example of choices that you'll encounter, you have to think about whether you need a permanent ink or not. Permanent inks (that usually come in pad form and are marked as "archival" inks) last indefinitely and won't run. On the other hand, they come in a limited number of colors and aren't as bright as regular pigment or dye-based inks. They work on any surface including paper, wood, and fabric. Crafter's ink is a thicker, permanent ink.

Most crafters use regular dye-based or pigment inks for stamping. These inks can be bought in the form of pads (that can be re-inked with bottled ink) or in bottles from which you can ink a blank pad. The pads are either felt or foam, and you'll find that dye-based inks usually come on felt pads, whereas pigment inks come on foam pads.

Dye-based inks can be used on all types of paper, but work best on coated, white paper. Pigment inks are opaque, thicker, slow to dry, and more resistant to fading than dye-based inks. They work well on uncoated paper and colored paper, wood, and terra-cotta. Their thickness makes them extremely effective to use with embossing powders (powders which are sprinkled onto the ink while it's wet before melting the powder with a heating tool). Pigment inks won't dry on coated stock unless they're embossed.

Similarly, embossing inks are designed to dry slowly. Unlike pigment inks, which are opaque, they come in transparent or translucent (with a hint of color

added) versions that allow colored embossing powders to show (photo 27). (If you plan to emboss pigment inks, use transparent or translucent powders so that the color of the ink won't be lost.) When using embossing powders, tap the excess powder onto a piece of paper so that you can pour the leftover powder into the container (photo 28).

Other permanent inks and paints are formulated for use on fabric and won't wash out when you launder the material that you've stamped. Most of these require that you wash the fabric beforehand to remove the sizing that can hinder the bonding of the ink and the fabric. After stamping, you'll probably need to heat set the stamped images. (Always follow the ink or paint manufacturer's directions exactly when stamping fabric that you plan to wash later.) If you plan to paint fabric that won't need to be washed (such as the face of a cloth doll or swatches of fabric in a collage) you can use almost any ink or paint for stamping.

You can effectively use a variety of paints for stamping. Acrylic paints (water-based paints traditionally used by artists that are akin to latex house paint) work well for stamping on most surfaces and dry quickly. They can be combined with other mediums such as transparent glazes and crackling mediums to create a number of surface effects and finishes. If you mix acrylic paints with textile medium, they become washable for use on fabrics.

Bottled water-based paints made for stamping come in a variety of colors as well as metallics. Because they stay wet longer than acrylic paints, you can apply several colors to a surface while they're still wet.

Stamping Surfaces

The most obvious surfaces for stamping are paper and fabric. A huge range of papers are available for purchasing, from handmade to commercial. For example, you can choose between coated and uncoated papers, textured and untextured, tissue and origami papers, vellum, and boards. Craft supply stores, stamp retailers, and stationery stores all carry an assortment of papers. Experiment with various inks and paints on papers, keeping in mind how different mediums behave on porous and non-porous surfaces (see Inks and Paints on pages 14 through 16).

Stamping on fabric has become increasingly popular and more accessible due to the variety of easy-to-use inks and paints on the market. Smooth weaves of cotton, cotton blend, muslin, linen, or silk in light colors are good fabrics for stamping. Don't forget to wash the fabrics beforehand (and iron them) if you plan to stamp them with permanent inks or paints.

You can stamp on almost any surface that will hold ink including an enormous variety of papers and fabrics. If you plan to stamp wood, you'll have more success with an unvarnished surface.

If you want to stamp wood, you might consider sticking with unvarnished wood (there are many unfinished wood pieces available at craft and home supply stores). Sand the surface of these pieces to remove inconsistencies, and leave the wood as it is or paint it with a coat of acrylic paint. Then you can use almost any kind of ink or paint for stamping (dye-based ink, pigment ink, permanent ink, crafter's ink, or acrylic paint). If you want to seal the surface, use an acrylic spray sealer.

To stamp on leather, expert leather crafter Kari Lee recommends using permanent, dye-based, or fabric inks sealed with two coats of leather sheen for the best results. (Always test out the results on a scrap of the leather that you plan to use.) There's no need to heat set inks that are used on natural leather or deerskin because the leather will be sealed. Some acrylic and fabric paints will crack and result in a rough surface. Adding a small amount of fabric medium to the paint helps.

Pigment inks don't dry well on leather, and tend to smear, unless they are embossed. You can emboss on leather with pigment or fabric ink and clear embossing powder.

After you've stamped a piece of leather (photos 29), you can color your design with markers (photos 30). Paint, watercolor, textile, and permanent markers can be used on leather and deerskin. (The color of watercolor markers tend to fade, however.) Sealing the surface will prevent the colors from bleeding.

Stamping without Ink

There are several stamping techniques that are commonly used in stamping to alter a surface without using ink or paint. If you haven't tried out some of these techniques and materials, you'll be compelled to do so after you see the wonderful results that they achieve. Look to the project section of this book for examples of how to use these techniques.

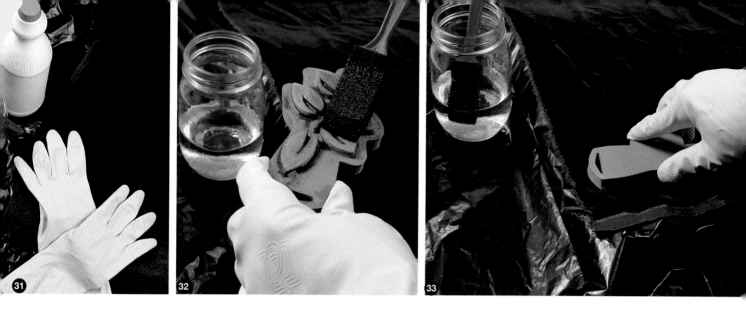

Stamping with Bleach

Using bleach to extract the dye from fabric can produce beautiful results that leave behind an impression of the stamp that you use. Different fabrics produce different results, and it's a good idea to test the fabric before you make a project. Try using cotton or velvet for good results.

To stamp fabric with bleach, you'll need a pair of rubber gloves, paper or plastic for covering your work surface, laundry bleach, a small glass container, a foam brush, a foam stamp, and fabric (photo 31). Open a window to provide good ventilation. Pour a small

amount of bleach into the glass container, and load the foam brush with bleach before applying it to the stamp (photo 32). Press the stamp onto a sample of your fabric, and hold it in place for several seconds (photo 33). The bleach will begin to fade the fabric gradually. Practice on the scrap fabric until you get the feel for how much bleach to use and how long to press the stamp. Keep in mind that applying too much bleach to your stamp can cause the fabric to bleed. Stamping on velvet can produce a ghostly impression of the stamp that is beautiful (photo 34), while stamping on dark cotton will produce a clearer image (photo 35).

19

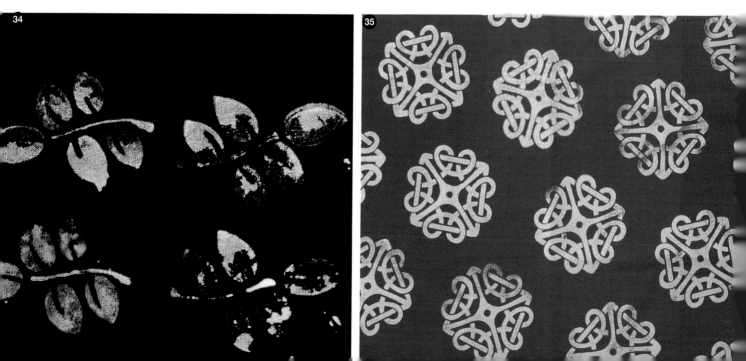

36

37

38

Embossing/Heat Stamping Velvet

Heat stamping velvet produces elegant, shimmering fabric for hats, scarves, pillows, or other items. This seemingly mysterious process is easy to undertake with a few simple materials.

20

First, choose a rubber stamp that has broad lines so that they won't get lost in the nap of the velvet. Rayon/acetate velvet works especially well for this technique, and cotton and silk velvet are good picks as well. (Avoid using nylon velvet.) You'll also need a clothes iron and a spray bottle with a mist setting filled with water (photo 36).

To begin, place the stamp faceup on your work surface, and then place the velvet facedown on the stamp (photo 37). Heat your iron to the "permanent press" setting. Spray the back of the velvet with a fine mist (photo 38). Place a sheet of paper on top of the covered stamp, and hold the iron in place for about 10 seconds (photo 39). Lift up the velvet to see if the nap is sufficiently pressed down to reveal a good impression (photo 40). Continue to mist and press to achieve a gorgeous, patterned fabric (photo 41).

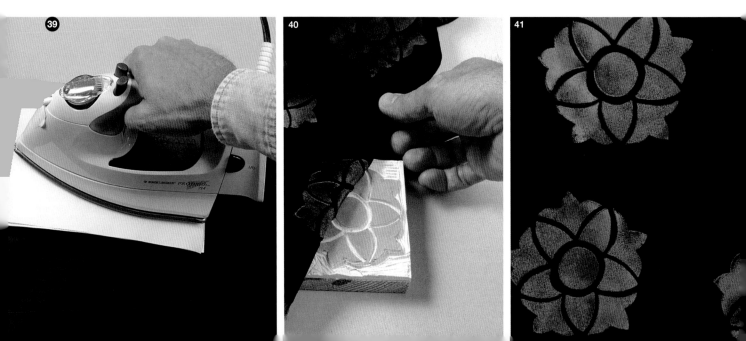

39

40

41

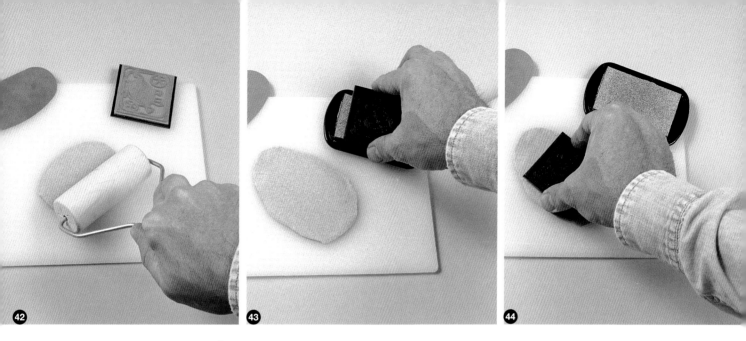

Stamping on Polymer Clay

Stamping on polymer clay can produce fascinating results. If you haven't worked with polymer clay before, stamping is a great way to introduce yourself to this versatile medium.

To stamp on polymer clay, you'll need a brayer or rolling pin for rolling out the clay, a rubber stamp with a rather broad design or one that is made for the purposes of stamping on clay, and a craft knife or slicing blade for trimming the clay after you've stamped it.

To begin, roll out a thin sheet of clay that is about ⅛ inch (3 mm) thick (photo 42). Ink the stamp with a contrasting ink if you'd like to make the image bold after you stamp it (photo 43). Press the stamp firmly and evenly onto the clay (photo 44). Remove the stamp to reveal your image (photo 45). Trim around the image with a knife or blade to create a small tile, a pin, or other item (photo 46). Bake the clay according to the clay manufacturer's instructions to harden the clay (photo 47). To further explore stamping on clay and the other techniques that we've just reviewed, turn to the extensive project section that follows.

21

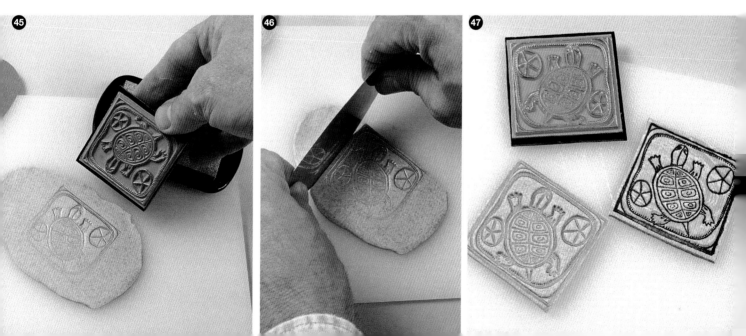

The Projects

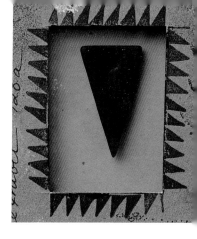

On the following pages you'll find 40 stamping projects from simple to complex for a variety of occasions and uses. To make any of these projects, you can closely follow our instructions or create your own interpretation of a designer's work with different stamps and color choices. In the back of the book is a list of credits for the commercial stamps that we've used, so you'll be able to order them or find them at your local craft store or rubber stamp store.

While undertaking your work in stamping, mix and match ideas that are brought forth, experiment, and, most of all, relax—this medium is easy and produces impressive results.

DESIGNER: Maggie Jones

Easy Leaf Prints

Use fresh leaves to stamp beautiful shapes on paper that can be embellished with paint, colored pencils, and other media.

YOU WILL NEED

Old newspapers

Fresh leaves in various shapes and sizes

Watercolor paper or other heavy, white paper

Acrylic paints

Sheet of glass, large ceramic tile, polystyrene food trays, or another flat, nonabsorbent surface to use as a palette for mixing paints

Palette knife or butter knife

Medium-sized round paintbrush or wedge-shaped foam applicator brush

Paper towels

Rubber brayer

Variety of media including watercolors, chalks, colored pencils, crayons, or other colored media of your choice

Fine-tip black marker

Scissors

White craft glue

INSTRUCTIONS

1. Cover your work surface with newspapers, and print several leaves on the paper with acrylic paint to form the background of your design. (See the instructions on page 10 for how to print with leaves.)

2. Randomly smear some of the excess acrylic paint on a piece of the newspaper. Put the paper aside to dry.

3. Apply streaks of watercolor or acrylic paint between the printed leaves to build your design.

4. If you wish, add more leaf prints on top of your design to create a layered effect. Allow the paint to dry.

5. Use chalks or other dry media to add more marks and color to your design.

6. Use a fine-tip marker to doodle designs in the areas of the paper that are left unfilled. Accent leaves or outline them with the marker as you wish.

7. Cut slivers from the scrap of painted newspaper, and collage them onto your design with glue as a final touch.

DESIGNER: Luann Udell

Lascaux Cards

This designer's work is inspired by the beautiful images of horses painted 17,000 years ago on the walls of the caves of Lascaux. Create your own small works of art by printing stamps on cards.

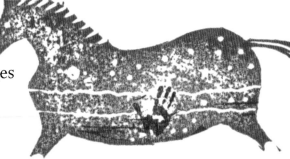

YOU WILL NEED

Cardstock pieces cut in half to measure
11 x 8½ inches (27.9 x 21.6 cm)

Dye-based ink pads in colors of your choice

Hand-carved stamps (see pages 10-12 for instructions)
or rubber stamps of your choice

INSTRUCTIONS

1. Fold the pieces of cardstock in half to form 5½ x 4½ inch (13.9 x 10.4 cm) cards.

2. Use your stamps and inks to print images of your choice on the fronts of the cards.

3. Combine various stamps in different ways to create a variety of images.

4. Sign the card with the title of your work of art, your name, and the date.

Embossed Notebooks

These gorgeous embossed notebooks are deceptively simple to make with the assistance of a nearby copy center. We embossed all of the stamped designs on the red notebook, and only the stamped pod designs on the green notebook—giving you a glimpse of how you can vary the look of the covers.

YOU WILL NEED

2 pieces of heavy board (illustration, book board, or mat board), each 8½ x 11 inches (21.6 x 27.9 cm)

Sponge wedge

Pigment ink pads in colors of your choice

Pattern stamps and accent stamps of your choice (see page 126 for the stamps that we used)

Embossing powders

Heat-embossing tool

½-inch (1.3 cm) stack of 8½ x 11-inch (21.6 x 27.9 cm) paper (computer paper, text weight paper, or other) for the inside of the book

INSTRUCTIONS

1. Use the sponge wedge to dab ink from one of the pigment ink pads all over the front of one of the boards to create a mottled effect. Allow the ink to dry.

DESIGNER: Judi Kauffman

2. Use pigment ink pads in colors of your choice to print rows of pattern stamp designs randomly or in a grid pattern. Add the prints of other stamps as accents.

3. Scatter embossing powders over the surface of your printed design to highlight as much or as little of the design as you want to. Set the embossing powder and inks with the heat-embossing tool.

4. Sandwich the stack of paper between the two book boards/covers.

5. Take the notebook to a copy center or printer that has binding services and have it spiral bound. Choose from the options available for colorful plastic-coated and regular metallic wires for your binding.

6. Add stamping inside the covers, if you wish.

DESIGNER: Kathy Anderson

Mona Lisa Altar

Choose a favorite icon (whether it's Mona Lisa, Marilyn Monroe, or your cat Mittens), and create a stamped and collaged altar in her honor.

YOU WILL NEED

Wooden triptych (available at craft supply stores)

Sandpaper

Tack cloth

Small, flat paintbrush

Acrylic paint in color of your choice for background

Translucent tissue paper made for wrapping

Decoupage medium or artist's acrylic medium

Scissors

Metallic thread

Rubber stamp of your choice (see page 126 for more information on the stamp that we used)

Kraft paper

Black permanent ink stamp pad

Art papers, wrapping papers, and interesting found papers

Small rectangular sheet of copper

Black pigment ink stamp pad

Black embossing powder

Heat embossing tool

Tacky glue

Small piece of plastic canvas (for stamping overall pattern)

Stickers, buttons, coins, and other embellishments of your choice

Paper clay

Ornate button or jewelry (for stamping clay)

Decorator chalks

Gold metallic ink stamp pad

Alphabet stamps

INSTRUCTIONS

1. Lightly sand and tack the wooden triptych. Paint both the inside and the outside of it with two coats of acrylic paint, sanding and tacking between coats. Allow the paint to dry thoroughly.

2. Tear and crinkle pieces of the translucent tissue paper to texturize them. Brush a coat of decoupage medium or acrylic medium onto the inside panels of the triptych. Randomly lay down pieces of the paper to create a collaged effect, and then brush a second coat of medium over the papers. (The medium acts as a glue.) Cover the outside of the triptych with tissue papers in the same manner.

3. While the medium is still wet, clip and randomly apply lengths of glittery metallic threads to the surface.

4. Use the stamp of your choice and black permanent ink stamp pad to print a series of images on the kraft paper. Alter the image by isolating various portions of it and printing it as a single image. (To do this, press or dab the ink on the portion of the stamp that you want to print and leave the other portions uninked before printing it.)

5. After the stamped images are dry, tear and/or cut around them to create smaller pieces of paper that contain the image. Cut and tear pieces from the art papers or wrapping papers to place behind the stamped papers. Layer the stamped papers and other papers to create a pleasing composition on the inside panels of the triptych. Adhere the papers by brushing a coat of medium on the

After the stamped images dry, tear or cut around them to create smaller pieces of paper that contain the image.

surface, pressing them in place, and then brushing a coat of medium on top of them. (Some thick papers may adhere better by dipping them in water before applying them.)

6. Use the same stamp to print an image on the sheet of copper with black pigment ink. Sprinkle on black embossing powder, and melt it with the heat embossing tool. Use tacky glue to adhere the copper to the inside of the triptych.

7. Press the piece of plastic canvas onto a black permanent ink stamp pad, and repeatedly stamp an overall design on the inside. When the ink is completely dry, apply stickers or glue on embellishments such as buttons or coins.

8. Flatten a small piece of the paper clay with your fingers. Press an ornate button or piece of jewelry into the clay to make an impression. Allow the clay to dry. Use tacky glue to add this textural piece to your composition.

9. Use the decorater chalks to enhance the edges of the papers, the background, and the paper clay.

10. Use your fingers to lightly rub gold metallic ink from the stamp pad over the surface of your composition.

11. Close the wings of the triptych. Cut out a rectangular piece of kraft paper that fits within the boundaries of the triptych. Cut it in half lengthwise. Brush a coat of medium on the back of the resulting papers, and press them into place on either side of the opening between the wings so that they relate to each other as a continuous piece. Use the alphabet stamps and the black permanent ink stamp pad to stamp words of your choice on them.

12. Adhere more papers of your choice, metallic threads, and stamped designs made with the plastic canvas to the outside of the triptych.

 Decorate the closed wings of the triptych with more papers and stamping.

DESIGNER: Justin Hawkins

Jazzy Wrapping Paper

Create intriguing gift wraps by carving your own stamps
before printing them on wrapping or kraft paper.
Stamp various colors on different papers to alter the design.

YOU WILL NEED

Drawing of your design for printing, or photocopy
of copyright-free artwork

Tracing paper

Transfer paper

Pencil or pen

4 x 6-inch (10.2 x 15.2 cm) rubber sheets made for
carving (available at art and craft supply stores)

Set of linoleum cutting tools
(available at art and craft supply stores)

Craft knife

Small blocks of scrap wood for stamp handles or
precut stamp handles

Epoxy glue specified for use with rubber

Brayer

Printing ink in colors of your choice

Sheet of glass, large ceramic tile, polystyrene food trays,
or another flat, nonabsorbent surface to use
as a palette for mixing inks

Scrap paper

Roll of plain wrapping paper or kraft paper

Tip: If you haven't carved with linoleum cutting tools before, try out
the various blades on a block of rubber to get a feel for the marks
that they make. Begin by carving basic designs. Don't try using too
many small details. The rubber pad cuts very easily, but must be
done with a sure and delicate hand. Always cut away from yourself.

INSTRUCTIONS

1. Trace the design that you plan to print onto tracing paper.
(Keep in mind that the final images will print in reverse.)
Place a piece of transfer paper between one of the drawings and the face of a rubber sheet. Trace the lines with a
pencil or pen. Remove the transfer paper, and check your
lines. Retrace any lines that aren't clear.

2. Use one of the carving blades to carefully remove the
rubber around the outmost edges of the design. Gouge
toward the edges of the block with the tool so that you
won't accidentally cut into the design. Keep in mind that
you're removing the rubber from areas that will remain white
when the stamp prints, and that the remaining raised surfaces will create the lines and shapes of the stamped image.

3. Switch the carving blades as needed to cut the details of
your design. Repeat steps 1 through 3 to carve as many
designs as you like.

4. Use the craft knife to trim away the excess rubber from
around the designs that you've carved. Choose a piece of
wood that has a face large enough to hold each stamp. Use
epoxy glue to adhere the stamps to their handles. Allow the
adhesive to dry thoroughly.

5. Roll out inks on the palette with the brayer and transfer
an even coat to each carved stamp. Experiment with the
printing of your stamps on pieces of scrap paper, varying
the placement and rhythm of your design.

6. Roll out your wrapping or kraft paper, and print the
designs in colors of your choice.

Altered Book

Transform an old book into a personal piece of art by adding your own collage, stamping, and words to enhance and reinterpret the book's pages.

YOU WILL NEED

Old hardcover book of around 100 pages or less

Medium-sized binder clips

Tacky glue

Materials for decorating the cover and the book pages: colored tissue papers, handmade papers, corrugated cardboard, gift wraps, pressed flower petals and leaves, threads and/or fibers, stickers, metallic paper ribbon, wire-edged ribbon, glitter, colored chalks, colored markers

Scissors

½-inch-wide (1.3 cm) flat paintbrush

Decoupage medium or artist's acrylic medium

Rubber stamps of your choice

Pigment or embossing ink pads in colors of your choice

Embossing powders in colors of your choice

Heat-embossing tool

Found objects to stamp with such as a polystyrene ball cut in half, rubber eraser, leaves, etc.

Cosmetic sponge

Paper doilies

Alphabet cookie cutters

1 yard (90 cm) of ½-inch (1.3 cm) colored ribbon

DESIGNER:

Kathy Anderson

34

INSTRUCTIONS

1. You'll begin altering your book by changing the number of pages that it has. If your book has 100 pages, for example, clip together every 10 pages with a binder clip. Remove the clip on each section and squeeze tacky glue between the inside pages before replacing the clip. Allow the sets of glued pages to dry with the book standing up. You'll end up with a book of 20 pages instead of 100, and these thick pages will serve as panels to decorate. After the pages have dried together, you'll notice that the book won't close completely.

2. Tear and crinkle pieces of the colored tissue papers. Brush decoupage medium on the book's cover, and press the papers into place, layering them as you go. Apply another coat of medium on top of the papers. (You'll notice that overlapping the tissues creates new colors).

3. Use the same technique to collage tissue paper and other materials of your choice to the inside pages. Allow the book to stand as it dries.

4. After the book has dried, use your rubber stamps and

stamp pads to begin adding designs to the outside and the inside of the book. Emboss some of them with powders using the heat embossing tool. Use found objects of your choice to stamp more designs onto the pages of your book.

5. Ink a cosmetic sponge, place a doily on one of your pages, and dab gold ink onto the face of the doily before lifting it off to create stenciled designs on your pages.

6. Dip the alphabet cookie cutters in pigment or embossing ink, and print letters on various pages of your book. As you go, highlight the letters with embossing powders, and melt them with the heat embossing tool.

7. Add more embellishment with fibers, glitter, and stickers. Color in areas of your designs with colored chalks and markers. If you wish, ink and emboss the sides of your pages.

8. Cut the yard (90 cm) of ribbon in half. Finish the cover with more collaged elements of your choice, and secure one of the ribbons underneath some collaged papers at the midpoint of the front cover. Repeat this process with the other ribbon on the back cover at its midpoint. After the papers have dried, tie the ribbon together as a finish for your book.

Collaged papers augment the pages of an old book to create new meanings.

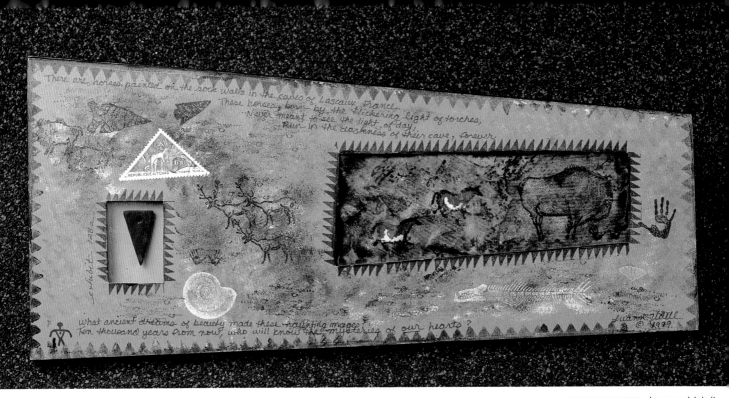

DESIGNER: Luann Udell

Stamped Mail Art

Send a collage through the mail that won't be ignored! This "giant postcard sandwich," as the designer calls it, is assembled in such a way that it will (probably) survive the mail system unscathed.

YOU WILL NEED

Metal ruler

Mat knife

Mat board in color of your choice

Pencil

Foamboard

Dark-colored masking tape or cloth tape

Wide-tip black marker

Sheet of clear plastic
(a report cover from an office supply store will work)

Masking tape

Collage components such as photos, letters, maps,
magazine pictures, newspaper clippings,
and small objects

Rubber stamps (including image, border,
and alphabet stamps) of your choice
(see page 126 for a list of the stamps that we used)

White craft glue

Double-sided tape

Permanent ink pads

Materials for decorating the outside of the piece: scraps of
colored paper or decorative papers cut with regular and
decorative-edged scissors, rubber stamps and inkpads,
small sponges and paint, cancelled postage stamps

INSTRUCTIONS

Note: The basic structure of this piece of mail art is made from two slices of mat board and the foamboard. Shallow insets for objects and collage are created by cutting windows in the foamboard, which are then covered with clear plastic for protection. The designer recommends creating the sandwich first before adding the collage elements so that an overall framework is established.

1. To begin, use the metal ruler and a mat knife to cut out a shape (such as a rectangle, square, triangle, or trapezoid) from the mat board. Your shape needs to be large enough to meet postal regulations, but small enough that it doesn't break your budget to mail it. Check with your post office for size restrictions. If your mail art piece is larger than a card, it is considered to be a "flat" by the post office.

2. Cut out a second identical sheet of mat board if you're cutting out a rectangle, square, or other regular-shaped form. If you're cutting out an odd shape, reverse the shape for the second piece by flipping the piece over and tracing around it before you cut it.

3. Cut out a piece of foamboard of the same shape but about ⅛ inch (3 mm) larger than the mat board pieces.

4. Think about what you plan to place in the windows (papers, artifacts, small objects, etc.). Decide on the size and placement of the windows in the finished piece, and sketch them onto the front of one of the pieces of mat board. Use the metal ruler and mat knife to cut out the windows. (The other piece of mat board will serve as the back wall of your piece.)

5. Place the cut mat board on top of the foamboard section, aligning the edges. Trace the windows with a pencil, and remove the mat board. Cut the windows out of the foamboard, enlarging them slightly so they won't show in the final piece.

Tip: How do you send such a thing through the mail? The designer notes that you're given a lot more latitude by the postal service if your piece is sturdy and devoid of sharp edges so it won't be destructive to other pieces of mail. Make sure your piece carries the necessary amount of postage, and you shouldn't have any trouble mailing it.

6. Line the edges of the windows on the foamboard with the dark-colored tape, so you can't see the white edges. Darken the white, inside edges of the windows on the mat board piece with the black marker. To protect each window, cut a piece of clear plastic about ½ inch (1.3 cm) larger than the openings, and tape it to the underside of the mat with masking tape.

7. Place the foamboard on the inside of the uncut piece of mat board (the back), and add objects, stamping, or collages inside each window.

8. Use craft glue to affix the artifacts in the windows. While the glue is drying, cover the outside edges of the foamboard with more dark-colored tape, and use the marker to color the outside edges of both mat board pieces.

9. When you've completed your stamping and collages inside the windows, place double-sided tape strips about ⅛ inch (3 mm) inside every edge (both outside and cut window edges) on both sides of the foamboard. Line up the edges carefully, and sandwich the three pieces together.

10. To decorate the front of the piece, rubber-stamp the edges with permanent ink and border designs. Add handwritten phrases, glue on cancelled postage stamps, or affix other paper components.

11. Decorate the back side of the piece, but leave plenty of space for an address and postage. If you own a small postage scale, weigh the piece to determine how much postage you'll need so you can plan the kinds of stamps you'll use. Otherwise, you can do this at the post office.

12. To address the work, use the alphabet rubber stamps. Be sure to write in your return address.

Tip: Incorporate "live" stamps of your choice into the design. Ask your postal person to show you a variety of stamps. To find stamps that are no longer current, contact a local stamp dealer by looking in the yellow pages or inquiring at antique and coin shops. You can use any postage that hasn't been cancelled. When you take the piece to a postal clerk, make sure that he sees each of the stamps so that it can be cancelled. You can also use foreign stamps purchased from stamp dealers that are live or cancelled as decoration on the piece. Ask dealers to see small packets of what are known as "topicals"—stamps that have similar themes such as flowers, insects, or fairy tales.

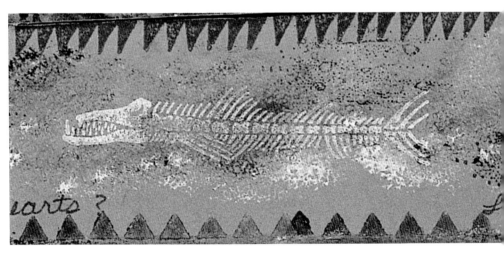

Accordion Book

This easy-to-make little book can serve as an elegant business card holder or repository for ticket stubs and other memorabilia.

YOU WILL NEED

Archival craft glue

Glue brush

2 pieces of decorative paper cut to 3¾ x 4½ inches (9.5 x 11.4 cm)

2 pieces of mat board or book board cut to 3½ x 4 inches (8.9 x 10.2 cm)

Ruler

Pencil

19 x 5½-inch (48.3 x 14 cm) piece of art paper for body of book

Bone folder

Mat knife or sharp scissors

Dye-based ink pads

Dragonfly rubber stamps or stamps of your choice (see page 126 for a list of the stamps used in this project)

Stipple brushes

⅛-inch (3 mm) hole punch

22 eyelets ⅛ inch, (3 mm) wide

Eyelet setting tool

24 inches (61 cm) of ½-inch (1.3 cm) ribbon

INSTRUCTIONS

1. Apply glue to the backs of the decorative papers with the brush, and press them into place on the pieces of mat board (you'll have a margin of paper around the edges). Wrap the margins of the papers neatly and tightly around to the backs of each piece of board. Burnish the papers well to be certain there are no air bubbles or wrinkles.

2. Use the ruler and a pencil to mark a line 1¾ inches (4.4 cm) from the bottom of the long edge of the piece of art paper. Use the bone folder to fold along this line to create the pockets for the book.

3. Fold the paper in half widthwise with the bone folder. Accordion pleat the paper at points 3 inches (7.6 cm) from this centerpoint on either side. Fold the paper once again at points 3 inches (7.6 cm) from the last pleats. (You should now have six paper panels.) Trim the outermost panels to 3 inches (7.6 cm) if needed. Crease each fold well with the bone folder.

4. Open out the long fold across the bottom of the paper. Cut the edge of the paper in a zigzag fashion from crease to crease.

5. Decorate the front and the back of the pages with stamps as desired. Stipple ink lightly onto the paper for added color.

6. Fold the bottom of the paper up again at the fold. Use the hole punch to punch a hole in each corner at the end where the folds overlap. Position and set a small eyelet in each hole with the eyelet setting tool. These eyelets should hold the folded paper in place at each end.

7. Place one of the covers facedown on your work surface. Center the length of ribbon over the middle of the cover, with a slightly longer piece to the right. Apply adhesive to the outside back page of the book, and center it over the back cover. Press them together so that the ribbon is contained by the back page and back cover.

8. Apply adhesive to the outside front page, and add the front cover. Place the booklet under a large book until dry.

9. Wrap the ribbon around the front cover, and tie it to hold the book closed.

Wrap the ribbon around the front, and tie it to hold the accordion book in place.

40

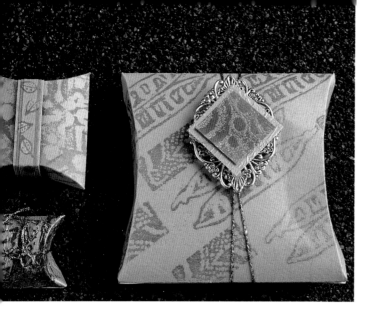

Decorative Pillow Boxes

Use a box template to cut out the pattern for a square pillow box, and stamp it before assembling it.

DESIGNER: Judi Kauffman

YOU WILL NEED

Photocopy of box template
(see page 124 for template, to order other patterns, see page 126)

Double-stick adhesive sheet or adhesive application machine with rollers

Card stock

Scissors

Small pattern and motif stamps
(see page 126 for the stamps we used)

Pigment ink pads in dark colors of your choice

Translucent embossing powder

Heat-embossing tool

Scoring tool

Bone folder

White craft glue

Gold gel pen (optional)

Decorative cord or ribbon (optional)

Dimensional embellishments such as charms, ribbons, rose, memorabilia (optional)

Wood excelsior (fine, curled wood shavings used for packing) or tissue to enclose your trinkets

INSTRUCTIONS

1. Adhere the photocopy of the box template to the card stock with a double-stick adhesive sheet or adhesive application machine. Cut out the box template. Don't score or fold the box at this point.

2. Use your stamps and pigment inks to print random designs on the front of the flattened box. Emboss the inks with translucent powder, and set with the heat-embossing tool.

3. Score the lines on the boxes with the scoring tool. Crease the folds with the bone folder. Fold and unfold them along the curved line so that the ends will snap into shape after the box is filled. Use white craft glue to glue together the box along the flap at the side.

4. To add a slip-on band to the box, cut a narrow piece of card stock long enough to fit around the closed edges of the box, and stamp it with a complementary design. Color the designs with the gold gel pen, if you wish. Place the band around the box, overlap the ends of it, and glue it into place.

5. If you don't use a card stock band, secure the box with cord or ribbon. Add embellishments to the ribbon if you wish.

6. Fill the box with tissue or wood excelsior, and small gifts or trinkets.

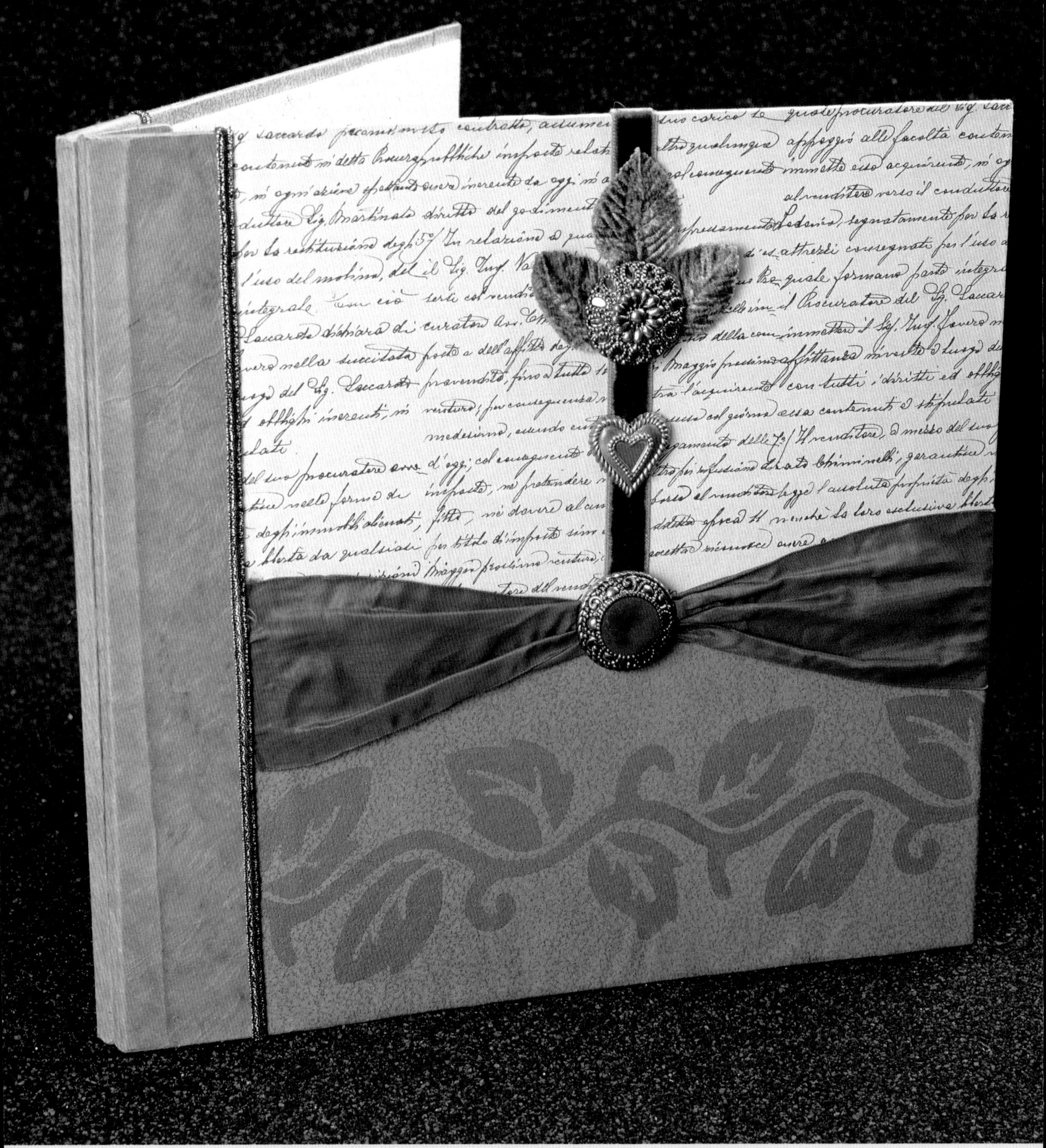

DESIGNER: Grace Taormina

Collaged Scrapbook

This designer capitalized on her love of papers, ribbons, and found objects to create this luscious scrapbook cover. By recycling materials from other projects, she combined her love of stamps and collage to make a one-of-a-kind scrapbook.

YOU WILL NEED

Assorted art papers and/or gift wraps

Assorted ribbons

Assorted buttons and other embellishments

Scrapbook

Scissors

Ruler

Foam stamps of your choice (see page 126 for information on the stamp that we used)

Gold acrylic paint or other color of your choice

Plastic-coated paper plate or polystyrene food tray to use as a palette

Wedge-shaped foam applicator brush

Double-sided adhesive paper

Archival craft glue

Glue brush

INSTRUCTIONS

1. Assemble interesting art papers and/or leftover gift wraps along with ribbons and embellishments. Play around with various combinations of the three for the cover of your book.

2. After you've chosen the items that you want to combine on your scrapbook cover, cut a piece of paper large enough to cover the top half of the cover plus 1-inch (2.5 cm) margin on the top and right edge. Cut another piece of paper for the bottom half of the cover, adding 1-inch (2.5 cm) margin to the right and bottom edge.

3. Place the papers on your work surface. Pour or squeeze a small puddle of acrylic paint onto your palette, and load the flat edge of the sponge brush with paint. Pat the paint onto a foam stamp in preparation for stamping.

4. Stamp the papers as you wish (it works well to use a large border stamp on the bottom, as we did). Allow the papers to dry.

5. Position the papers on the cover with the 1-inch (2.5 cm) margins on the top, side, and bottom. Notch the corners of the papers, and fold back the margins of the papers to the back of the board. Adhere the papers with double-sided adhesive paper (cut to the size of the papers) or archival craft glue and brush, smoothing them as you go, and folding the margins around to the back of the cover.

6. Use glue to adhere strips of ribbon to the cover as well as buttons or other embellishments.

YOU WILL NEED

Shipping tag

Dye-based ink pads in colors of your choice

Gibson girl, pattern stamps, and heart-shaped seedpod stamps (see page 126 for ordering information)

Colored pens or markers

White craft glue

3 leaf beads or charms

Piece of card stock

Scissors

⅛-inch (3 mm) hole punch

6-inch (15.2 cm) piece of narrow, colored ribbon

Stamped Gift Ensemble

Stamp on die-cut, pre-scored card stock pieces with a Gibson girl theme and assemble them into a variety of small gift boxes, hanging ornaments, or gift tags.

Gift Tag

Use a variety of stamps that carry the same theme to make a matching gift tag.

INSTRUCTIONS

1. Lightly press the face of one of the ink pads onto the shipping tag to print a background on which to stamp.

2. Press ink of another color onto the Gibson girl stamp, and print it in the center of the tag, about ⅜ inch (9.5 mm) from the tag reinforcement.

3. Stamp pattern stamps at the corners of the tag. Randomly print the heart-shaped seedpod stamp on the tag.

4. Use colored pencils or markers to add color to the face, hair, and skin of the Gibson girl design.

5. Glue three leaf beads or charms below the tag reinforcment.

6. Glue the tag onto a piece of card stock, and cut it out, leaving a narrow border. Punch a hole in the card stock to reopen the hole in the shipping tag.

7. Loop and tie the narrow ribbon through the tag's hole.

Hanging Lantern Ornament

Tint the background of the card stock pieces before you stamp them to create an antiqued look.

YOU WILL NEED

Gibson girl cherub rubber stamps
(see page 126 for ordering information)

5 die-cut "lantern" card stock pieces
and 2 pointed top/bottom sections
(see page 126 for ordering information)

Paper towels

Dye-based ink pads in colors of your choice

White craft glue

9-inch (22.9 cm) piece of narrow ribbon for hanging loop

12-inch (30.5 cm) piece of 1½-inch-wide (3.8 cm) wire-edged organza ribbon

INSTRUCTIONS

1. Stamp images on all of the card stock pieces.

2. Dab a paper towel onto the ink pad, and apply color to slightly tint and antique the five stamped side pieces as well as the top and bottom pieces.

3. Follow the manufacturer's instructions to assemble the lantern ornament with craft glue.

4. Attach the narrow ribbon to the top as a hanging loop. Tie a soft wire-edged ribbon bow, and glue it to the top in front of the hanging loop.

Whispering Cherub Box

Stamp with fine-lined stamps and add color with pencils to decorate a charming box.

YOU WILL NEED

6 die-cut and pre-scored "lantern" style card stock pieces
(see page 126 for ordering information)

Gibson girls cherub, and heart-shaped seedpod rubber stamps (see page 126 for ordering information)

Dye-based ink pads in colors of your choice

Colored pencils

White craft glue

Wood excelsior (fine, curled wood shavings used for packing) or tissue paper

Small gifts and trinkets

INSTRUCTIONS

1. On four of the card stock pieces, use stamp pads to print a design with the Gibson girl cherub and heart-shaped seedpod stamps. Stamp seedpods only on the remaining two pieces that will serve as the lid and bottom.

2. Color in the Gibson girl images with colored pencils.

3. Following the manufacturer's instructions, glue together the four side pieces and the box bottom. Glue the lid on by one of the flaps to form a hinge.

4. Fill the box with wood excelsior or tissue, and add small gifts and trinkets.

DESIGNER: Nicole Luperini

Tag Art

Convert a luggage tag into a small work of art with rubber stamps and inks.

YOU WILL NEED

5 x 7-inch (12.7 x 17.8 cm) piece of fabric for background

5 x 7-inch (12.7 x 17.8 cm) piece of mat board

Fabric glue

4¾ x 2⅜-inch (12 x 6 cm) manila shipping tag

Rubber stamps including pattern stamps, image stamps, phrase stamps, and number stamps (see page 126 for a list of the stamps that we used)

Dye-based or permanent ink pads in colors of your choice

Pigment or embossing ink pad in color of your choice

Embossing powder

Heat-embossing tool

Small tassel

Scissors

12-inch (30.5 cm) piece of fabric trim

Hot glue gun

Button

⅔ yard (61 cm) of fabric fringe

INSTRUCTIONS

1. Adhere the piece of fabric to the mat board with fabric glue.

2. Invert the shipping tag so that the hole is at the bottom.

3. Next, you'll print a series of stamps, allowing the ink to dry between each step. To begin, use one of the dye-based or permanent ink pads and a pattern stamp to stamp the shipping tag's background with an overall design.

4. Layer stamped images on the tag until you arrive at a design that you like.

5. Use the pigment or embossing ink pad to stamp images before embossing them with embossing powder. Melt the powder with the heat embossing tool.

6. Slip the loop of the tassel through the hole of the tag, and use fabric glue to adhere the tag (with the hole at the bottom) to the center of the fabric-covered mat board.

7. Cut four strips of trim to fit around the edges of the tag and attach them with the hot glue gun. Hot glue a button over the loop of the tassel and the hole of the shipping tag.

8. Flip the piece over, and cut four pieces of fringe to fit around the edges of the backside of the piece. Overlap the strips at the corners to give the fringe fullness. Hot glue the strips around the edges of the backside of the mat board, so that they serve as a frame when you look at the piece from the front.

Elegant Paper Boxes

It's hard to believe that the stamps for these sophisticated boxes began as pieces of rubber baseboard.

YOU WILL NEED

Pieces of rubber baseboard
from a home supply store
(1 for each stamp you'd like to carve)

Small section of no-slip foam rubber shelf liner

Set of linoleum carving tools

Craft knife

Two-sided, waterproof tape

Block of polystyrene insulation cut to a size
that fits your baseboard stamp

Ruler

2 sheets 8½ x 11-inch (21.6 x 27.9 cm)
heavyweight construction paper or card stock

DESIGNER: Emily Wilson Hintz

Scissors

Bone folder

Acrylic paint in colors of your choice

Small sheet of glass or a large dinner plate

Foam roller

Decorative edging scissors (optional)

White craft glue

Paintbrush

Wax paper

INSTRUCTIONS

1. Transfer a sketch or image to the baseboard by following the directions on page 12 or leave the baseboard unmarked if you prefer to carve your stamp directly.

2. Place the section of no-slip shelf liner underneath the baseboard to keep it from slipping while you carve it.

3. Use the linoleum carving tools to cut away portions of the stamp that will not be inked (see instructions on pages 11 and 12). Repeat this process if you'd like to use more than one stamp on your box.

4. Use the craft knife to trim the edges of the baseboard stamp. Use the two-sided, waterproof tape to attach the carved stamp (or stamps) to the polystyrene insulation. (The insulation is lightweight and makes an easy-to-clean handle for your stamp.)

5. Use the scissors to cut out one 8-inch (20.3 cm) square (for the box) and one $5\frac{5}{8}$-inch (14.3 cm) square (for the lid) from the construction paper or card stock. Save the paper scraps for later.

6. Cut out a 2-inch (5.1 cm) square from one corner of the 8-inch (20.3 cm) square. Trace the outline of this paper square at the other three corners, and cut out three more squares. Cut a 3/4-inch (1.9 cm) square in one corner of the $5\frac{5}{8}$-inch (14.3 cm) square, and repeat the same process. After you're done, you should have four flaps on these papers to form the box and the lid. Crease each of the flaps with the ruler, and then score them with the bone folder.

7. Squeeze small dollops of the acrylic paints on the sheet of glass or dinner plate. Blend them together slightly as you smooth them with the foam roller to create a gradated palette. Roll an even coat of paint onto your stamp or stamps.

8. Place the pieces of your box (including the tabs) flat on your work surface. Stamp one side of the pieces, allow them to dry, and then stamp the other side. Add another layer of stamping to your design if you want.

9. Use the scraps of paper that you saved in step 5 to make corner tabs. Cut four 2 x 1-inch (5.1 x 2.5 cm) lengths for the box and four $\frac{3}{4}$ x 1-inch (1.9 x 2.5 cm) lengths for the lid from the leftover paper. Fold each tab in half lengthwise. Trim the flaps with the decorative edging scissors if you want. Stamp the tabs with a design, paint them, or leave them plain.

10. Place one of the 2-inch (5.1 cm) tabs on the wax paper, and brush the back of it with a coat of glue to give an even application. Bring two adjacent flaps of the box together (stamped side out), and secure them with the tab to form the first corner. Secure the other three corners of your box with the remaining tabs. Repeat this process to secure the sides of the lid of the box with the smaller tabs.

49

Use common rubber baseboard, polystyrene insulation, and carving tools to make a simple but effective stamp.

Hanging Book

The idea for the unusual structure of this book was devised by the designer. Beautiful stamped and collaged surfaces are hidden inside until they are folded out to reveal the whole design.

DESIGNER: Kinga Britschgi

YOU WILL NEED

3 pieces of 4½-inch-square (11.4 cm) decorative paper for the covers

3 pieces of 3½-inch-square (8.9 cm) mat board for covers

Archival craft glue or glue stick

Glue brush (if using craft glue)

Ruler

2 pieces of 1 x 3-inch (2.5 x 7.6 cm) black card stock for the binding

3 pieces of 3¼-inch-square (8.2 cm) colored foil

2 pieces of 4-inch-long (10.2 cm) black organza ribbon, approximately ½ inch (1.3 cm) wide

Strong, double-sided tape

25-inch-long (63.5 cm) piece of black silk cord

3 pieces of 3 x 15-inch (7.6 x 38.1 cm) black card stock

Asian-themed rubber stamps of your choice (see page 126 for a list of the stamps we used)

Gold metallic stamp pad

Papers with Asian theme (such as Chinese Jost papers)

³⁄₁₆-inch (4.8 mm) hole punch

3 brass eyelets, each ¼ inch (6 mm) wide

Eyelet setting tool

Thin brass wire

Wire clippers

3 small pebbles or other small weights

Jewelry or round-nosed pliers

Small bead, about ⅜ inch (9.5 mm) in diameter

INSTRUCTIONS

1. Miter the edges of the decorative papers to fit the three pieces of mat board. Use the craft glue or glue stick to adhere the papers to the boards.

2. Flip the covers over, and connect them inside with the two black card stock pieces. To do this, place the three covers in front of you leaving about a ¼-inch (6 mm) gap between them. Center a black card stock strip over each of these gaps so that they connect the neighboring covers, and glue them into place.

3. On each back cover, center and glue a piece of colored foil in place to cover the board.

4. Fold the black organza ribbons in half. Attach the looped ribbons with strong double-sided tape placed at least ⅝ inch (1.6 cm) from the top of the two outer-most boards (they'll need this strength for hanging the book later).

5. Use double-sided tape to attach the silk cord horizontally to the inside of the right cover in the center. Set aside the covers.

6. To create the hanging accordion pages, fold each 3 x 15-inch (7.6 x 38.1 cm) piece of black card stock into a five-piece accordion (each section will be a 3-inch [7.6 cm] square).

7. Stamp the accordion pages with rubber stamps and gold metallic ink, and glue on bits of oriental papers to make a collage.

8. Use the hole punch to punch a hole on the bottom of each of the accordion pages. Attach an eyelet in each hole.

9. Wrap lengths of brass wire around each pebble, and leave a tail of about 5 to 8 inches (12.7 to 20.3 cm) at the end. Attach the pebbles to the eyelets at different lengths by stringing half of the wire tail through each hole. Reinforce the wire by doubling and twisting it, using the pliers when needed. (When you open and hang the book, these rocks will serve as weights.)

10. Use double-sided tape to attach the top panel of each accordion page to one of the covers.

11. String the bead onto the silk cord from step 5, and tie a knot at the end of it to prevent the bead from slipping off.

12. To close the book, fold up each of the accordion pages, and fold in the left cover first. Then fold the right cover over it. Wrap the cord around the book several times, and loop it under itself.

13. To hang the book, open it back up and use the ribbon hangers.

This unusual book is closed by folding in the left and right wings before wrapping a cord around it.

DESIGNER: Kinga Britschgi

Masked Magnets

Use a simple masking techique to integrate stamped images into designs that transform everyday items into objets d'art.

YOU WILL NEED

Cutting mat or pile of newspapers

Craft knife

Pencil

Sheets of plain paper

Masking tape

Rubber stamps with motifs of your choice
(see page 126 for information on the stamps we used)

Black permanent ink stamp pad

Blank sticker sheets (one side is sticky)

Black, fine-tip permanent marker

Watercolor pencils

Small paintbrush

Scissors

Magnetic sheets
(available at craft supply stores)

Spray varnish or fixative

INSTRUCTIONS

1. Place the cutting mat or a thick layer of newspapers on your work surface. Use the craft knife to cut out a piece of plain paper that measures approximately 3 x 4 inches (7.6 x 10.2 cm). Draw a 2 x 3-inch (5.1 x 7.6 cm) rectangle inside, and cut it out with the craft knife. (This piece of paper will serve as a mask or frame for your design.)

2. Place the paper mask in the center of a piece of plain paper, and use masking tape to hold it in place on the top edge.

3. Choose three to five rubber stamps with which to build your image within the frame. Experiment on plain paper with the stamping, and don't worry about overlapping the edges of your frame.
(**Tip**: To stamp a background behind an image without it interfering with the image, print the image on a piece of paper, cut it out, and place it where you want it in the frame. Leave it there as a mask when you print the background stamp [such as the text]. Remove the paper mask, then print the image in the blank space.)

4. Try out several compositions on paper with your frame. (When you are happy with the results, you can transfer these ideas to the paper that you'll use to make your magnets.)

5. Cut out clean paper frames for each of the magnets you plan to create. Tape each frame into place on a sticker sheet, and stamp images with black permanent ink, using your test designs as a reference. When every element is stamped, remove the masks. With a black, fine-tip marker, draw a line around the natural edge of the design.

6. Use watercolor pencils to color the images. Limit the number of colors that you use, and allow the black lines and foreground elements to dominate. Use a small paintbrush and some water to blend the colors as you wish.

7. When you're satisfied with the result, use scissors or the craft knife to cut out each image, leaving a small border of blank paper around the edges. Peel off the backing of the sticker paper, and attach the pieces to the magnetic sheet. Cut out the magnets with the craft knife. Spray a coat of varnish or fixative onto the surface of the magnets to protect them.

DESIGNER: Tana Boerger

Ceramic Platter

Stamp a piece of bisqueware with simple materials at your nearest contemporary ceramic studio, and the studio will glaze and fire it for you.

INSTRUCTIONS

1. Collect fresh leaves from your yard.

2. Take the leaves and a piece of mesh carpet pad to your nearest contemporary ceramic studio (a studio that will provide you with the bisqueware and underglazes, as well as fire the ceramic piece for you).

3. At the studio, pick out a piece of bisqueware that you like, and several underglazes to use on the piece.

4. Squeeze one of the underglazes onto a blank ceramic tile, and dab the piece of carpet padding with the color. Repeatedly transfer the print of the pad onto the background of the bisque.

5. Paint the back of one of the leaves with another underglaze. Press the leaf onto the surface of the bisqueware. Repeat this process with other leaves to create a design that you like.

6. Embellish the piece (by painting the rim) if you wish. Leave the piece at the studio to be fired and glazed.

YOU WILL NEED

From home:

Fresh leaves

Small square of mesh carpet padding

Provided at the studio:

Bisque platter of your choice

Underglazes in several colors

1 or 2 blank ceramic tiles

Small paintbrush

DESIGNER: Maggie Jones

Leaf Napkins

Go no further than your own backyard for some of the most interesting stamping materials around.

YOU WILL NEED

Cotton napkins

Iron

Old newspapers or newsprint

Sheet of glass, large ceramic tile, polystyrene food trays, or another flat, nonabsorbent surface to use as a palette for mixing paints

Red, yellow, blue, black, and white fabric paints

Palette knife or butter knife

Medium-sized round paintbrush or wedge-shaped foam applicator brush

Fresh leaves in various shapes and sizes

Paper towels

Rubber brayer

INSTRUCTIONS

1. Wash and dry the napkins to remove the sizing, and press them out with the iron.

2. Cover your work surface with old newspapers or newsprint. Place the palette on the work surface, and apply small amounts of each of the fabric paints. Use the palette knife or butter knife to mix up colors of your choice (for instance, combine yellow and red to make orange, blue and red to make purple, and yellow and blue to make green). Add white paint to colors to lighten them and black paint to darken them.

3. After you've mixed some colors that you like, use either the paintbrush or a foam brush to apply a thin, even coat of one of the colors to the backside of one of the leaves.

4. Since some leaves print better than others, practice printing the leaf on a piece of newspaper so you can see how the leaf will print. (You can use a leaf several times.) After placing the leaf painted-side-down on the paper, cover it with a paper towel. Roll the rubber brayer back and forth with light pressure over the leaf to distribute the paint. Carefully pull up the leaf by its stem.

5. If you like the way the leaf prints, repaint it, and print it on one of the napkins using the same technique.

6. Continue this process to add leaf imprints to the rest of your napkins. (Before overprinting, allow each of the prints to dry thoroughly.) Be spontaneous with the colors you use and the designs you create.

7. After you've finished your designs and the paint has dried thoroughly, heat set the paint by ironing the napkins with a medium-hot iron. Wait a couple of days before washing the napkins in warm water for the first time.

Children's Shoe Bag

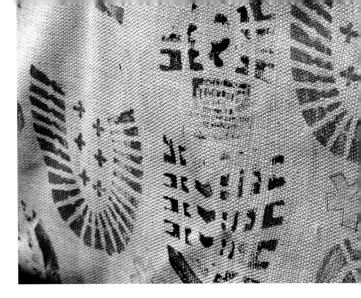

Stamp a shoe bag with intentional shoe prints (not the kind that you have to scrub off the carpet!). You'll be amazed at the smart-looking results.

YOU WILL NEED

Newspapers or newsprint

Children's shoes with bold, treaded soles
(use shoes that you don't mind getting paint on, such as those from a thrift store or ones that your children have outgrown)

Fabric paints of your choice (we used black, brown, white, bronze, copper, and silver)

Disposable polystyrene food trays, egg carton, or other palette

Wedge-shaped foam applicator brush

Shoe bag made of light fabric (a printed fabric will work if the design is not too dark)

Old book or piece of board that is slightly smaller than the width of the shoe bag's pockets

Alphabet-shaped stamps

INSTRUCTIONS

1. Place a layer of newspapers or newsprint on your work surface.

2. Place the shoes and stamps on your surface. Squeeze out puddles of the fabric paints onto the palette. Use the foam brush to apply a coat of paint to the treads of one of the shoes.

3. Situate your shoe bag so that the surface that you are about to print is flat. If needed, hold the book or board inside the shoe bag with one hand while you press with the other from the outside.

4. Press the inked tread of the shoe firmly onto the bag. (Don't worry if the tread doesn't print perfectly, this is part of the charm of the design.) Use the other shoes and alphabet stamps to randomly stamp a design in various colors onto the fabric, overlapping prints as you go. Don't be afraid to be experimental! Cover as much of the bag with prints (inside and outside) as you wish. (You may need to print one area of the bag at a time, and allow it to dry before printing the next.)

DESIGNER:
Sandy Donabed

Velvet Pillow

A stamp loaded with bleach is used to lift the dyes from velvet and leave behind shimmering impressions on this pillow's surface.

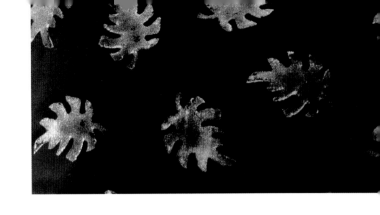

DESIGNER: Camille Gibson

YOU WILL NEED

½ yard (45.7 cm) of 100% cotton velvet in a dark color

Fabric scissors

Iron

Mild detergent

Old sheet or towel

Plastic trash bag

Rubber gloves

Bleach

Small glass container

Foam tipped applicator brush

Foam stamp of your choice or stamp made from recycled materials (see page 101 for instructions)

Rag or paper towels

Straight pins

Dressmaker's pencil

Sewing machine and thread

4 black silky tassels

Pillow stuffing

Sewing thread and needle

INSTRUCTIONS

1. Wash, air-dry, and gently press the velvet on the wrong side. (Be careful not to press too hard, or you may leave an impression on the nap.) Cut out two 16¾-inch (42.5 cm) squares.

2. Fill a kitchen or bathroom sink with mild detergent and warm water.

3. Open a window in your work space for ventilation. Place an old folded sheet or towel on your work surface, and cover it with the plastic trash bag.

4. Place a leftover scrap of the velvet, right side up, on top of the padded surface. Put on your rubber gloves.

5. Pour a small amount of bleach into the small glass container. Dip the foam-tipped applicator brush in the bleach, and swab it onto the stamp. Use a rag or paper towel to blot away excess bleach that runs down the handle.

6. Press the stamp firmly into the nap of velvet, and hold it for approximately five seconds. Don't worry if you splatter the bleach; this can create an interesting effect. Allow the bleaching process to progress until you like what you see. The longer you leave the bleach on, the lighter your image will become, revealing the base color of your fabric. When the fabric reaches a stage that you like, stop the process by rinsing the fabric in the warm, sudsy water followed by a rinse of clear water.

7. Place one of the 16¾-inch (42.5 cm) squares of velvet faceup on the padded surface. Work at a steady pace, pressing your stamp at even intervals on the face of the velvet, and turning it to vary the design. If you want, you can leave the other square blank and have it serve as the "back" of your pillow, or you can stamp and bleach it with the design. After your designs have reached the desired look, rinse the velvet in warm, sudsy water, and rinse it with clear water before hanging it to dry.

8. After the velvet dries, gently press it with an iron on the wrong side. Place the right sides of the two pieces together, and pin them together every inch (2.5 cm) or so on all four sides within a ⅝-inch (1.6 cm) seam allowance. (Avoid pinning beyond this seam, because the pins may leave marks in the velvet.)

9. Use a dressmaker's pencil to make a dot ¾ inch (1.9 cm) from each corner of the wrong side of the velvet square.

10. Stitch three sides together, stopping about 1/8 inch (3 mm) before each corner dot. Do the same on the fourth side, but leave about 4 inches (10.2 cm) of the seam unsewn for the purpose of turning the pillow later.

11. Insert a tassel inside each corner of the pillow where you marked a dot. Pin the tassel in place, and stitch across the corners.

12. Turn the pillow right side out, and fill it with pillow stuffing. Turn the edges of the open seam inside, and whipstitch the pillow closed by hand.

DESIGNER: Grace Taormina

Overprinted Pillow

Because of her love of exotic, faraway places, this designer is partial to home decor items with an international flair.

YOU WILL NEED

Old newspaper or other scrap paper

Fabric scissors

½ yard (45.7 cm) of patterned fabric in color and design of your choice

½ yard (45.7 cm) of dark, solid-colored fabric for back of pillow

Masking tape

Fabric paints in colors of your choice (we used black, dark red, and mustard)

Plastic-coated paper plate or polystyrene food tray to serve as palette

Several sponge wedges

Broad-based foam stamps
(see page 126 for information on the leaf and fossil stamps that we used for this project)

Buttons or other embellishments of your choice

Needle and thread (optional)

2 yards (1.8 m) of decorative fringe (optional)

Straight pins

Sewing machine and thread

Pillow stuffing

INSTRUCTIONS

1. Protect your work surface with layers of old newspaper or other scrap paper. Use the fabric scissors to cut out a 14 x 16-inch (35.6 x 40.6 cm) piece of patterned fabric for the front of the pillow and a 14 x 16-inch (35.6 x 40.6 cm) piece of solid fabric for the back of the pillow.

2. On the patterned fabric, use masking tape to cover any areas that you don't want to overprint (we masked off the solid mustard-colored line on our pillow).

3. Pour a small puddle of paint in a color of your choice onto the plate, food tray, or other palette. Load the flat edge of a sponge wedge with paint, and dab the paint onto the first stamp that you plan to use.

4. On the right side of a scrap of leftover printed fabric, over-print your first stamp to try it out. Change the color of the paint if it doesn't read well. Try out any other stamps and colors that you plan to use.

5. After trying out your stamps, apply your design with the stamps to the front of the patterned fabric. Apply fresh paint every time you stamp, and press the stamp firmly overall.

6. Allow the paints to dry thoroughly, and remove any tape that you may have used. If you're adding buttons or other embellishments, use a needle and thread to sew them into place on the front of the pillow.

7. Place the right sides of the back and front of the pillow together, and match the edges. If adding fringe, insert it between the front and back along the edges, allowing it to rest inside the two pieces of fabric. Pin the fabric pieces and fringe together, making sure that the fringe is evenly aligned with the edges. Clip off any extra fringe so that the two ends meet. Sew together all four sides with a 5/8-inch (1.6 cm) seam, leaving about a 4-inch (10.2 cm) opening so that you can turn the pillow inside out.

8. Clip off the excess fabric about ¼ inch (6 mm) from the seam at the corners of the pillow. Turn the pillow inside out, and stuff it. Slipstitch the opening and the fringe into place to complete the pillow.

DESIGNER: Kari Lee

Plush Botanic Cushions

These gorgeous leather pillows show off elegant stamped designs.
Make the square pillow described below, or alter the design to
make a rectangular pillow.

YOU WILL NEED

FOR SQUARE PILLOW

Tan deerskin (see page 126 for supplier)

Smoke deerskin (see page 126 for supplier)

Leather shears

Contact cement made for leather

Large binder clips

Craft knife and additional blades

Poster board

Ruler

Pencil

Mini hole punch set (available at craft supply stores
or from supplier on page 126)

Multi-colored dye-based ink pad

Leaf-shaped stamps and other rubber stamps
for center design
(see page 126 for a list of the stamps we used)

Black dye-based ink pad

Watercolor or fabric markers
in a range of colors

Aerosol leather sheen

Pounding board to protect work surface
(see page 126 for supplier)

Fine-tip black marker

$\frac{3}{8}$-inch (9.5 mm) and $\frac{9}{16}$-inch (1.4 cm) parachute spots

$\frac{3}{32}$-inch (1 mm) lacing chisel and polymer head mallet (see
page 126 for supplier)

Leaf pattern stamp for pillow background
(see page 126 for the stamp we used)

Terra-cotta dye ink pad

1 yard (90 cm) of decorative fringe

Sewing thread to complement fringe

100/16 leather needle for sewing machine
(available at sewing supply store)

Sewing machine

"Deertan" cowhide (see page 126 for supplier)

16-inch (40.6 cm) square pillow form

INSTRUCTIONS

1. Use the leather shears to cut out a 17-inch (43.2 cm) square pillow front from the tan deerskin.

2. For the back pillow cover, (which will be made of two overlapping pieces with an envelope-like opening), cut out one trim piece from the tan deerskin that measures 8½ x 17 inches (21.6 x 43.2 cm) and a second piece that measures 10 x 17 inches (25.4 x 43.2 cm). Overlap these two pieces to create a 17-inch (43.2 cm) square. Use the contact cement to baste together the joining outside edges. Secure the edges with the binder clips while the leather dries.

3. To create a pattern as a guide for punching the holes along the envelope opening for lacing later (see step 13), use a craft knife to cut out a 4 x 17-inch (10.2 x 43.2 cm) piece of poster board. Use the ruler to mark a center line down the length of the board before marking the positions of 14 parallel holes that are spaced 1 inch (2.5 cm) apart along each side of the line. Attach the largest tube of the mini hole punch set in the drive handle, and punch the holes out on the pattern. Line up the center line of the pattern with the overlapping leather seam (envelope opening), and punch holes on either side where indicated by the pattern.

4. Cut out a piece of smoke deerskin that measures 9 inches (22.9 cm) square. Place the square of leather faceup on your work surface, and use a multi-colored ink pad to thoroughly ink the square, patterned stamp that you plan to use in the center of the pillow. Stamp the image in the center of the leather square.

This close-up view of the pillow shows the strength of its central design.

5. Using the finished project as a design guide, thoroughly ink the remaining leaf stamps with black ink and print them.

6. Add additional color to the stamp images with markers by layering green, yellow, and blue (you might want to test out the markers on a scrap of leather first).

7. After all of the stamping and color has been completed and has dried, the leather must be sealed. Spray a light coat of leather sheen onto the stamped leather, in order to condition the leather with a flexible, durable water-repellent finish.

8. Using the finished pillow as a guide, make tiny dots on the pillow front with a fine-tipped black marker where you'd like to attach the metal studs, or parachute spots. With the pounding board, press the prongs of each spot onto the leather at these points until they leave impressions. Using the impressions as a guide, make small incisions with the lacing chisel and mallet. Push

the prongs of each spot through the leather, and use the end of the chisel to fold the spots' prongs down on the backside, securing them in place.

9. On the 17-inch-square (43.2 cm) pillow front, use the larger stamp and the terra-cotta ink pad to print a repeating pattern around the edges, covering about a 4-inch (10.2 cm) border around the sides. After it dries, apply a light coat of leather sheen to protect the ink.

10. Center the stamped 9-inch-square (22.9 cm) leather piece on the pillow front, and secure it with cement. Use the cement to lightly secure a line of fringe along the seamline of the square. To permanently secure the fringe, machine-stitch it in place with the leather needle.

11. To assemble the pillow cover, clip the right sides of the pillow front and back cover together with a binder clip. Machine-stitch a ½-inch (1.3 cm) seam with the leather needle along all four sides of the pillow cover.

12. To reduce the bulk of the corners, trim them with the leather shears. Finger press the seam allowances open. Apply a thin, even amount of cement to the underside of each seam allowance. Press the seams into place, and allow the cement to dry. Turn the pillow right side out, and insert the pillow form.

13. To make the leather lace needed for the closure of the pillow back, cut a 12-inch (30.5 cm) circle from "deertan" cowhide. With leather shears, cut a ½-inch (1.3 cm) width of leather lace by following the circumference of the circle to create a spiral. Cut until you've cut about a yard (90 cm) of lace. Thread the lace through the holes on the back, crisscrossing them like shoelaces. Once the seam is completely laced, tuck the excess lace inside the pillow cover.

A repeating pattern made with the same stamp enhances the sides of the pillow.

DESIGNER: Lynn B. Krucke

CD Clocks

Before you toss out those junk CDs that you get in the mail, consider making them into functional works of art. Two versions of this clever idea are described below, but the possibilities are endless.

YOU WILL NEED

for TIME FOR ART *motif*

Junk CD

Small paintbrush

Artist's gesso or primer

Sea sponge (available at art or beauty supply stores)

Ivory, cream, and ecru acrylic paints

Assorted rubber stamps including number stamps
(see page 126 for a list of the ones we used)

Crackle stamp
(four-sided stamp with different sizes of crackle)

Black, light gray, and brown ink pads

Decorative paper for the back of the clock

Pencil

Scissors

White craft glue

Sheet of plain paper

Fender washer (a large washer available
at home and hardware stores)

Clock movement and hands

INSTRUCTIONS

1. Paint the front of the CD with several coats of gesso or primer. Allow it to dry.

2. Use the sea sponge to apply several shades of acrylic paint to achieve a mottled effect. Allow the paint to dry.

3. Stamp the surface of the CD randomly with rubber stamps and inks, allowing images to overlap and run off the edges. Stamp numbers around the edges.

4. Ink the crackle stamp with light gray ink, and stamp it repeatedly all over the CD.

5. Trace the outline of the CD onto a sheet of decorative paper, and cut it out with the scissors. Glue it to the back of the CD. Poke a hole in the paper to accommodate the clock mechanism.

6. Trace the fender washer onto a sheet of paper. Cut out the circle, then paint and stamp it to complement the CD. Glue it onto the washer.

7. Install the clock mechanism according to the manufacturer's instructions, adding the washer to the front to compensate for the large hole in the CD.

Time for Art This designer wanted to remind herself to take time out everyday for making art. The end result is an inspiring reminder!

CD Clocks

YOU WILL NEED

for AUTUMN'S GLORY *motif*

Discarded CD

Fender washer (a large washer available at home and hardware stores)

Artist's gesso or primer

Small paintbrush

Green and blue patinas (each patina consists of a metal laden paint [copper, bronze, or iron] and a patina [copper sulfate] that oxidizes the paint— they are available at craft supply stores)

Paintbrush

Sea sponge

Leaf and number rubber stamps

Permanent black ink pad

Decorative paper

Glue

Clock movement and hands

INSTRUCTIONS

1. Paint the fronts of the CD and the fender washer with several coats of gesso or primer. Allow them to dry.

2. Apply several coats of copper metallic paint/surfacer to the primed surfaces of the CD and washer. While the final coat is still tacky, dribble on green and blue patinas.

3. Once the patinas have developed, apply permanent black ink to the leaf stamp with the sea sponge. Stamp a leaf repeatedly on the surface, then stamp numbers at the 12, 3, 6, and 9 o'clock positions.

4. Cut out a circle of decorative paper for the back of the clock and adhere it to the back. Poke a hole in it for the clock mechanism.

5. Install the clock mechanism according to the manufacturer's instructions, adding the washer to the front to compensate for the large hole in the CD.

Autumn's Glory

Capture the ephemeral nature of fallen leaves on a timeless timepiece.

Classical Art Calendar

Overlapping stamped images with classical references elevate this calendar to the realm of art.

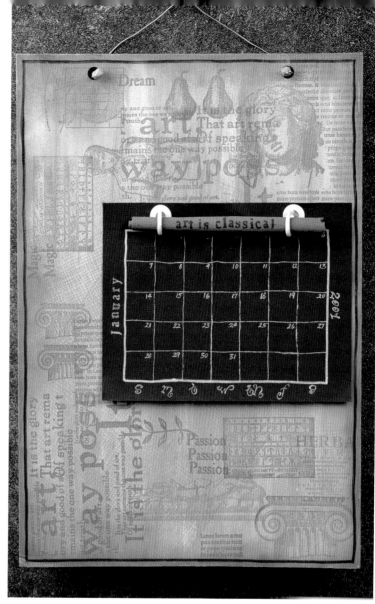

DESIGNER: Kinga Britschgi

YOU WILL NEED

9 x 13-inch (22.9 x 33 cm) piece of heavy white or light-colored mat board

Watercolor paints

Watercolor brush

12 pieces of 6 x 5-inch (15.2 x 12.7 cm) black cardstock (for calendar pages)

Ruler

Silver gel pen

Small set of alphabet stamps

Silver metallic stamp pad

¼-inch (6 mm) hole punch

Round page reinforcers

Pencil

Awl or icepick

5-inch-long (12.7 cm) twig

Acrylic paint (optional)

Black pigment ink pad

Rubber stamps of your choice
(see page 126 for a list of the stamps we used)

Dye-based or pigment stamp pad in color that complements your background color

Black wide-tip marker

2 small beads

9-inch (22.9 cm) piece of thin wire

Jewelry or round-nose pliers

2 decorative cords, each 4 inches (10.2 cm) long

INSTRUCTIONS

1. Paint the background of your mat board with the watercolor paints, using long, wide strokes. Don't cover the board completely, but leave evidence of your strokes. Set aside the board, and allow the paint to dry.

2. Assemble the pieces of black cardstock. On each page, leave about a ½-inch (1.3 cm) margin on all sides, and draw a grid of 35 squares (seven horizontal and five vertical) with the silver gel pen.

3. Use the silver pen to write in the numbers of the days and abbreviations for the days of each month, using a calendar for the year you're documenting as a guide for placement. Use the alphabet stamps and silver metallic stamp pad to print the name of the month on the left-hand side of each sheet of the calendar.

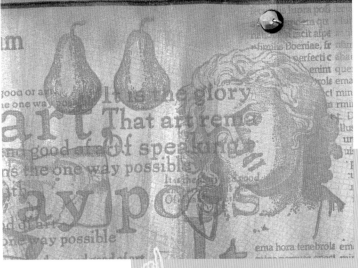

Layer stamp images to create interesting collage-like images.

4. Use the hole punch to punch two holes 1½ inches (3.8 cm) from each side and ½ inch (1.3 cm) from the top on each of the sheets. Make sure to punch all the holes in exactly the same places. Stabilize the holes with round page reinforcers.

5. Position one of the monthly pages on the background board wherever you like. Mark the position of the two holes with a pencil. Lightly outline the page. Using an awl or icepick, poke holes through the board at the pencil marks.

6. Paint the twig with a coat of acrylic paint or leave it natural. Use the black pigment ink pad and alphabet letters to print a phrase of your choice on the twig.

7. Try out your rubber stamps on a piece of scrap paper, layering them to create interesting collage-like designs. Repeat motifs to create rhythm. After you decide on a general idea for a design, stamp the mat board with a variety of stamps and ink in a color of your choice.

8. After you've finished stamping, dab the watercolor brush on the silver metallic stamp pad, and paint long silver streaks on top of your design. After the coloring has dried, use the wide-tip black marker and the ruler to draw a rectangular border close to the edge of the mat board.

9. Use the awl or ice pick to punch two holes in the top of the board that are 2 inches (5.1 cm) from each side and ½ inch (1.3 cm) from the top.

10. String one of the two beads on the end of the wire. Use pliers to bend the wire around the base of the bead so that it won't slip off. Push the other end of the wire through one of the holes at the top of the board so that the bead rests on the front and won't slip back through. Push the beadless end of the wire through the other hole from the back of the board to the front. Slip on the other bead, and bend the wire around the base of it with the pliers so that the bead won't slip back through the hole. Bend the wire in the middle so that it forms a hanger.

11. Fold each of the cords in half. From the back of the board, push the looped ends through the holes to the front. Slide the calendar onto the cords, and rest the twig inside the loops. Pull the cords tight from the back, and tie a knot in each of them to hold the pages and the twig.

12. To remove a month from your calendar after you begin using it, slide out the stick, pull off the page, and then replace the stick.

70

Goddess Clock

Egyptian motifs are stamped on paper and embossed on copper to adorn the face of an elegant clock.

DESIGNER: Kinga Britschgi

YOU WILL NEED

Compass

Pencil

Sheet of card stock in reddish brown or other color of your choice

Decorative-edged scissors with ragged edge

Script stamps

Moss green pigment ink pad or color of your choice

Sienna pigment ink pad or color of your choice

2 image stamps of your choice to mark the four quadrants of the clock
(see page 126 for the stamps that we used)

Stamp positioner (optional)

Several word stamps of your choice
(see page 126 for the stamps that we used)

Charcoal pigment stamp pad

Thin copper sheet, about 8 inches (20.3 cm) square

Metal shears or old pair of scissors

Cyanoacrylate glue or industrial-strength adhesive

Piece of mat board or heavy cardboard to use as backing

Mat knife

Awl

Image stamp for center piece of clock that measures about 3 inches (7.6 cm) in diameter
(see page 126 for the stamp that we used)

Soft surface such as an old mousepad

Medium-sized dry-embossing tool

Clock movement and hands

INSTRUCTIONS

1. Use the compass and pencil to draw an 8-inch (20.3 cm) circle on the piece of card stock to form the clock face. Cut out the circle with decorative-edged scissors to give the paper a ragged edge.

2. Use the large script stamp and moss green ink to stamp a script pattern onto the clock face. Stamp the script several times, using the centerpoint of the clock to determine the position of your stamp as you stamp it in quadrants. Use the stamp positioner, if needed.

3. Use your compass (set at the centerpoint of the face) to draw a 7-inch (17.8 cm) circle inside the outside edge of the face.

4. On the face of the clock within the 7-inch (17.8 cm) circle, use the sienna-colored pad (or other color) to stamp one of the image stamps in the 9 and 3 o'clock positions, and the other image stamp in the 12 and 6 o'clock positions. Leave a space in the center for adding a foil piece later. Use a stamp positioner if needed.

5. Stamp words of your choice in charcoal at the 12, 3, 6, and 9 o'clock positions.

6. Use the compass to draw a 7-inch (17.8 cm) circle on the copper sheet. Follow this by drawing a 6-inch (15.2 cm) circle within the larger one. Cut out this 1-inch-wide (2.5 cm) circular piece with a pair of metal shears or an old pair of scissors.

7. Cut out sections of various sizes from the circle every ¼ inch (6 mm) or so in the direction of the centerpoint of the circle.

8. Arrange the pieces around the edge of the clock face in line with the penciled circle that you drew in step 3. Once you are pleased with the arrangement of the pieces, glue them into place.

9. Draw a 7-inch (17.8 cm) circle on the piece of mat board or cardboard. Cut it out with the mat knife. Use the awl to punch a hole in the center of it. Line up the hole in the clock face with the hole in the backing, and glue them together.

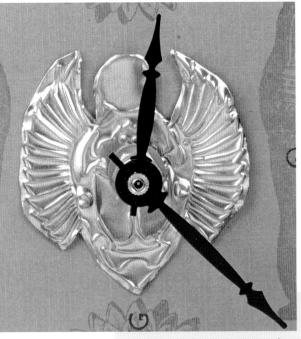

A dry-embossed copper sheet makes an eye-catching center for this clock.

10. With the charcoal ink pad, print another image stamp (with about a 3-inch [7.6 cm] diameter) onto a left-over piece of the copper sheet. Allow it to dry.

11. Place the sheet on a soft surface, such as an old mousepad. Use your dry-embossing tool to trace the lines of the image, pressing gently to emboss the metal. When you're done, flip the piece over and cut it out along the bordering lines with metal shears.

12. Use the awl to poke a hole that is about 3/8 inch (9.5 mm) wide in the middle of the clock face. Repeat this process on the embossed centerpiece.

13. Glue the embossed piece in the center of the clock face, making sure that you line up the two holes. Allow the glue to dry overnight.

14. Follow the manufacturer's instructions for attaching the clock mechanism through the center holes. Enlarge the hole with your awl, if needed.

DESIGNER: Lynn Damelio

Celtic Knot Table Topper

The inspiration for this gorgeous table topper came from a vintage batik tablecloth found in a quaint antique store. Instead of using wax as a resist, as it is in batik, bleach is used in this project to extract the pigment from the fabric, leaving behind a ghost impression of the stamp image. The results are as beautiful as they are easy to achieve.

YOU WILL NEED

Newsprint or kraft paper

2 yards (1.8 m) of red cotton fabric

1 yard (90 cm) of black cotton fabric

Fabric scissors

Bleach

Small glass container

Foam-tip applicator brush

Celtic knot foam stamp
(see page 126 for information on the stamp
that we used for this project)

Plastic-coated paper plate
or polystyrene food tray for use as palette

Gold textile paint

Wedge sponge

Straight pins

Black sewing thread

Sewing machine and thread

Iron

3 yards (2.7 m) of black and gold ribbon trim

4 black fringed tassels, each about 3½ inches
(8.9 cm) long

Sewing needle and thread

INSTRUCTIONS

1. Work in a room that is well ventilated (open a window if you can). Protect your work surface with several layers of newsprint or kraft paper. From the red cotton fabric, cut a piece that measures 24 inches (61 cm) square and one that measures 30 inches (33 cm) square. From the black fabric, cut two strips that measure 4 x 30 inches (10.2 x 76.2 cm) and two strips that measure 4 x 24 inches (10.2 x 61 cm). Save the leftover scraps for practicing.

2. Pour a small amount of bleach into a glass bowl. Dip the foam-tip applicator brush in the bleach, and pat it onto the surface of the foam stamp.

3. Press the stamp onto a scrap of the red fabric for several seconds and look at the result. The bleach will start to fade the fabric gradually. Practice on the scrap fabric until you get the feel for how much bleach to use and how long to press the stamp. Keep in mind that applying too much bleach to your stamp can cause the fabric to bleed.

4. Beginning in the center of the square of red fabric, create a design by stamping the knot design with the bleach. Space each print a couple of inches (5.1 cm) from the next one and work your way across the fabric. Allow the design to bleed off the edges of the fabric. When you've finished, set the fabric aside to dry. Rinse your stamp with water, and dry it off.

5. Pour a small amount of the gold textile paint onto the paper plate or food tray. Load the paint onto the flat edge of the wedge sponge. Pat the paint onto the stamp.

6. Practice stamping the gold paint onto a scrap of the black fabric until you achieve a print that you like. Stamp the black fabric strips with the knot design, and set the fabric pieces aside to dry.

7. After the pieces have dried, assemble the four stamped black strips, the red stamped square, and the unstamped red square of fabric. Pin the two shorter black strips to two opposite ends of the stamped red square, stamped sides together. Sew the strips to the square with ⅝ inch (1.6 cm) seams. Press the seams from the back so that the two strips are folded out.

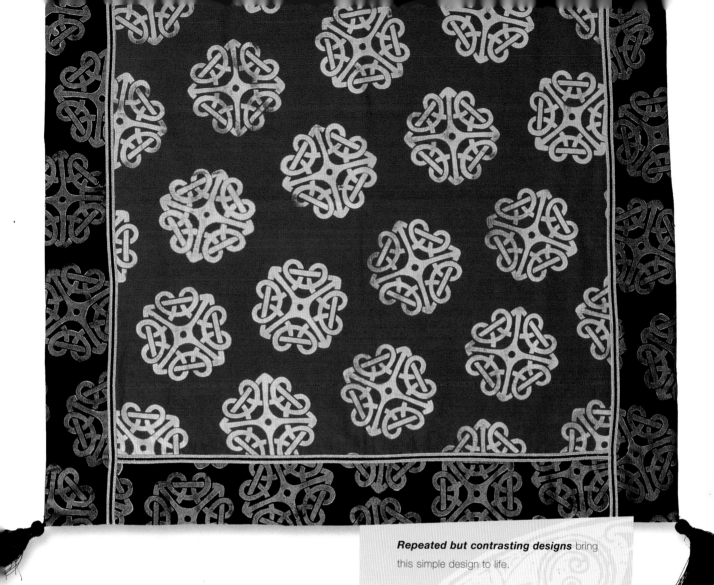

Repeated but contrasting designs bring this simple design to life.

8. Pin the two longer black strips to the other sides of the red square, stamped sides together. Sew them onto the square with ⅝ inch (1.6 cm) seams. Press them out from the back.

9. Sew trim on top of the two shorter seams. Then sew trim on top of the two longer seams, overlapping the ends of the trim that you sewed on top of the short seams.

10. Pin together the right sides of the unstamped red square and the large stamped and assembled square. Sew a ⅝-inch (1.6 cm) seam all the way around the edges, leaving about 3 inches (7.6 cm) unsewn so that you can turn the fabric like you would if you were making a pillow.

11. Turn the stamped fabric to the front, and press the seams along the edges. Sew the tassels by hand to the corners of the topper.

DESIGNER: Karen Timm

Elegant Evening Purse

The sensuous surface of this elegant purse is stamped with repetitive patterns in a shade of ink that is only slightly lighter than the fabric.

YOU WILL NEED

15-inch (38.1 cm) length of midweight fabric with a satin or glossy finish (40 to 45-inch [101.6 to 114.3 cm] width)

Fabric scissors

2 photocopies of pattern (page 124)

24-inch (61 cm) length of fabric adhesive

Fabric tape

Fabric marking pencil

Ruler

Rotary cutter

Self-healing cutting mat

Iron

18 x 25-inch (45.7 x 63.5 cm) sheet of plastic

Water or oil-based fabric paint in white and brown

2½-inch-wide (6.4 cm) hard rubber brayer

Sheet of glass, large ceramic tile, polystyrene food trays, or another flat, nonabsorbent surface to use as a palette for mixing inks

Palette knife

Small and large pattern stamps that complement one another (see page 126 for the stamps that we used)

Stamp positioner (optional)

1 yard (90 cm) of taupe-colored decorative cording

Sewing machine

Double-sided adhesive tape

1-inch (2.5 cm) piece of adhesive-backed hook and loop tape

INSTRUCTIONS

1. Press the fabric, and fold it in half widthwise. Use the fabric scissors to cut out two 15 x 22-inch (38.1 x 55.9 cm) pieces. Save the rest of the fabric for the lining.

2. Place the printed side of the pattern down on the paper side of the fabric adhesive, leaving at least a ½-inch (1.3 cm) margin around the edges. Hold the pattern in place with fabric tape. Trace around the pattern (including the cut marks) with the fabric marking pencil and the ruler. Remove

the pattern, and use the rotary cutter and mat to cut ½ inch (1.3 cm) outside the pencil line, keeping the pencil line intact.

3. Place the cutout piece of fabric adhesive facedown on the wrong side of the fabric (with the penciled paper side facing you). Heat press them together on a low to medium setting for 10 seconds. (Note: it helps if you first hold the paper with one hand while the other quickly and lightly slides the iron over the whole paper to get an even, overall contact.) Lift the iron to the next position, and repeat for 10 seconds, until all the areas are bonded. Allow the fabric to cool.

4. Cut along the traced pencil line, keeping the edges straight and clean. Clip into the edge flaps and corners where noted, but not past the lines. Peel the paper off, and keep it for later use. Be careful not to lift off any adhesive or fray any edges. Set the piece aside.

5. Cut out the second pattern, and trim away all of the flaps, leaving the tab intact. Place the pattern faceup on the wrong side of the remaining taupe fabric. Use tape to hold the pattern in place on the remaining fabric (which will serve as your lining fabric). Lightly trace along the edge of the pattern, using a ruler and marking pencil.

6. Remove the pattern, and cut out the lining with the rotary cutter, keeping the edges as clean as possible. Set aside the lining.

7. Cover your work space with the sheet of plastic, and tape it down. Place the scraps of your purse fabric on it, as well as your palette, inks, brayer, and palette knife.

8. Mix together some white fabric paint with a touch of brown until you achieve a color that is slightly lighter than your fabric. Roll the paint out on the palette with the brayer,

and roll an even coat onto your stamp. Experiment on your scraps with the stamping, and practice aligning the prints in a row.

9. When you're ready, use the larger stamp to begin printing from the center of the front of your purse with a row of designs that runs from one end to the other. (Use a stamp positioner to keep your line straight, if needed.) Continue to print the stamp to the left and to the right to form a grid pattern until you print the entire piece.

10. Ink and use the smaller stamp to print designs between the ones that you've already printed. Set the purse aside to dry.

11. Place the wrong side of the lining on top of the adhesive side of the purse fabric. Use saved pieces of the paper backing to mask the adhesive on the edge flaps before pressing the lining to the purse (using the same process as described in step 3).

This simple stamp creates an elegant repeating-pattern motif on this purse. (see page 126 for stamp credit).

12. Remove the paper pieces and turn in the edge flaps in the order noted on the pattern. Sandwich an inch (2.5 cm) of each end of the cord into the side flaps where noted, before turning the flaps in. Add small strips of double-sided adhesive tape for better adherence, and press the flaps into place.

13. Sew a double seam across the center of the purse.

14. Cut a 3/8-inch (9.5 mm) square of hook-and-loop tape, and adhere it to the inside of the right flap. Fold the right flap in, and adhere another closure to the outside of the purse and on the inside of the longer flap so that the purse closes.

DESIGNER:

Karen Timm

Swank Velvet Hat

Before you make this elegant hat, heat emboss the velvet with stamps to make it shimmer.

YOU WILL NEED

Photocopy of hat pattern (see page 125)

Straight pins

Fabric scissors

1/3 yard (30.5 cm) of rayon/acetate velvet (avoid nylon velvet)

1/3 yard (30.5 cm) of lining fabric

Craft knife

Broad-based rubber or foam stamp (or stamps)
of your choice with a simple design that will
emboss easily (see page 126 for the stamps we used)

Piece of scrap velvet

Spray/misting bottle

Iron

Sewing needle

Matching thread

Sewing machine

Needle board

INSTRUCTIONS

1. Cut out the patterns (sideband, brim, and crown), and wrap the sideband around your head to determine the length that you need to cut. Add a ½-inch (1.3 cm) seam allowance to this length. Fold the velvet as shown in the pattern, pin the pattern pieces in place within the seam allowance (so that pin marks on the velvet won't show later), and cut them out.

2. Repeat this process to cut out pieces from the lining fabric.

3. Use the craft knife to cut away any excess rubber or foam that surrounds the stamps, so that it won't affect the imprint of the design on the velvet.

4. Place your stamp faceup on your work surface, and lay the piece of scrap velvet, right side down, on the face of the stamp. Fill your spray/misting bottle with water, and lightly mist (don't saturate) the area of the fabric that is directly over the stamp. Turn the iron on a high or cotton setting, and place it directly on the velvet-covered stamp, avoiding the steam holes in the face of your iron (they'll leave marks). Press it for about 20 seconds. Lift up the iron to be certain that you've imprinted the entire stamp.

5. After practicing on the scrap, stamp the velvet crown in the center with the process outlined in the previous step.

6. Stamp designs on the top half of the velvet sideband below the top seam allowance area and 1½ inches (3.8 cm) above the bottom edge (so that the folded brim won't cover up your designs later).

7. Stamp across the velvet brim, rotating the stamp left and right as you go.

8. With the right sides together, sew the velvet sideband together on the short end. Finger press the seam open.

9. With the right sides together, pin the velvet

This close-up shows the crisp detail that can be achieved with heat embossing.

sideband to the velvet crown. (Be careful to place the pins in the seam allowance only.) Baste $3/8$-inch (9.5 mm) from the raw edge. Remove the pins, and machine sew together with a $1/2$-inch (1.3 cm) seam. Remove the basting thread, and trim the seam to a $1/4$-inch (6 mm) seam.

10. With the right sides together, pin the sideband and crown lining together, leaving about a 4-inch (10.2 cm) opening unsewn for the purpose of turning the hat later.

11. With the right sides of the velvet together, sew the 3-inch-wide (7.6 cm) end seam of the brim together. Repeat this step with the brim lining.

12. With the right sides together, pin, then baste, the velvet brim to the lining around its outside curved edge. Remove the pins.

13. Sew a $1/2$-inch (1.3 cm) seam along the brim's outside curved edge. Trim the seam to $1/4$ inch (6 mm). Turn the brim right side out. With the velvet side facedown on the needle board, press the lining edge of the seam. (The needle board prevents the nap of the velvet from being crushed.)

14. Attach the brim to the hat by pinning the lining side of it to the right (velvet) side of the hat's sideband, matching up all three raw edges and seams. Baste the brim to the sideband through all three layers. Remove the pins, and sew a $3/8$-inch (9.5 mm) seam.

15. Place the right side of the sideband and crown lining in place on the right side of the hat. Pin the raw edges together, and sew a $1/2$-inch (1.3 cm) seam with the velvet

The stamps for this project come in a neat box (see page 126 for stamp credit).

81

side facing up on your machine, so you can make sure there are no puckers in the velvet. Trim the seam to $1/4$ inch (6 mm).

16. Turn the hat inside out through the opening left in the lining.

17. With the velvet side of the brim on the needleboard, iron the lining side of the seam that you just sewed.

18. Turn in a $1/2$-inch (1.3 cm) seam allowance in the lining opening, and slipstitch it closed with a needle and thread. Tack the lining to the velvet in the seam allowances between the top and the sideband.

DESIGNER: Judi Kauffman

Airy Scarf

Use a simple air-propelled pen to blow permanent color onto a knotted scarf and create random, elegant patterns. Untie the scarf, stamp it with feathery images, and you'll be dazzled by the results.

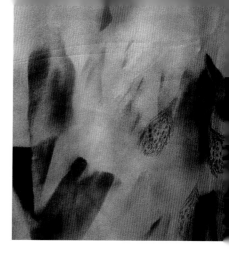

YOU WILL NEED

Old newspapers or newsprint

Plastic bags

Several air-propelled pens from which you can blow out permanent color in black, yellow, brown, and orange (available at craft stores)

Scrap of old cotton garment or scrap of silk

Dye-ready long white silk scarf
(Note: dye-ready silk has no sizing or finish on the fabric and will accept color readily. If you don't have dye-ready fabric, prewash and iron your scarf before coloring it.)

Finely detailed feather and seed stamps
(see page 126 for a list of the stamps that we used)

Iron

INSTRUCTIONS

1. Cover your work surface and surrounding area with layers of newspaper or newsprint and plastic bags. (The permanent colors from the pens that you will be using dry quickly and create a permanent stain.)

2. Practice using the air-propelled pens on a scrap of fabric before beginning the project.

3. Loosely pleat the scarf, and tie it in a knot every few inches.

4. Blow the color from a black pen randomly onto the knots, the pleats, and the gathers.

5. After the color dries, untie the knots. Iron the scarf to remove any wrinkles, and heat set the color according to the manufacturer's instructions.

6. Blow yellow, brown, and orange (or any colors desired) between the black areas, fanning the color out to give it a feathery effect. Blow more color at the ends of the scarf, and leave lots of white toward the center. Heat set the color.

7. Ink the rubber stamps with color from the tips of the pens. Quickly add designs to the scarf with the stamps—the ink dries fast! Stamp feathers or seedpods in one direction, or allow them to scatter in a random pattern. Heat set the colors with an iron.

Golden Pear Purse

Stamp cut fabric with designs of your choice, and stitch up a one-of-a-kind bag. The following instructions will enable you to construct a purse in any size that you choose.

DESIGNER: Lynn B. Krucke

YOU WILL NEED

½ yard (45.7 cm) of cotton fabric for the outer purse

½ yard (45.7 cm) of complementary or coordinating cotton fabric for lining

Fabric scissors

Measuring tape

Newsprint or other paper to protect work surface

Fabric paints in colors of your choice

Plastic-coated paper plates or polystyrene food trays

Wedge sponges

Foam stamps or other broad-based stamps without a lot of detail

Iron

Sewing machine

Coordinating thread

1 yard (90 cm) of multi-strand cording for strap

Sewing needle

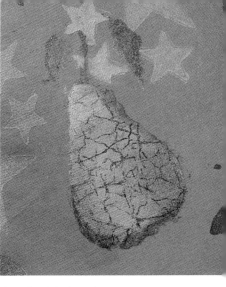

INSTRUCTIONS

1. Wash and iron the fabrics to remove all traces of sizing.

2. Decide on the finished height and width of your purse. For the outer fabric, cut a piece that is your desired width plus 1 inch (2.5 cm) by two times your desired height minus 1 inch (2.5 cm). Cut the lining fabric the same width as the outer fabric by two times the height plus 3 inches (7.6 cm). (This additional lining fabric will be used as a band around the top of the purse.)

Example: For a finished purse measuring 7 inches (17.8 cm) wide x 9 inches (22.9 cm) long, you'd cut the following: outer fabric: a rectangle measuring 8 inches (20.3 cm) wide x 17 inches (43.2 cm) long; lining fabric: a rectangle measuring 8 inches (20.3 cm) wide x 21 inches (53.3 cm) long.

3. Protect your work area with a layer of newsprint or other paper. Pour small amounts of each fabric paint to be used onto plates or trays.

4. Apply the paint to the stamps with wedge sponges, being careful not to get paint into the crevices of the stamps. To create blended colors, apply more than one color of paint to a stamp with the wedges. Practice on a scrap of the outer fabric to confirm that the colors and images suit you.

5. Fold the outer fabric in half with the raw edges of the width at the top. Visualize this folded fabric as the finished purse, and stamp a design of your choice on the front and back. Press each stamp firmly on the fabric, and lift it carefully to prevent smudging.

6. Allow the fabric to dry thoroughly once it has been stamped. Follow the manufacturer's instructions for heat setting the fabric paints.

7. Fold the right sides of the stamped fabric together, and stitch up the sides with a ½-inch (1.3 cm) seam. Sew up the sides of the lining fabric, leaving approximately 2 inches (5.1 cm) open along one of the sides.

8. Turn the lining so that the right side faces out. Place the lining inside the purse so that the right sides of the purse and lining touch and the top edges match.

9. Stitch the lining to the purse along the top edge with a 1/2-inch (1.3 cm) seam. Once the top edge is completely stitched, pull the lining out of the purse and turn the purse through the hole left in the side of the lining.

10. Once the purse is turned, whipstitch the opening in the lining closed, and reposition the lining inside the purse. Because the lining was cut longer, the joining seam will be approximately an inch (2.5 cm) from the top of the purse, and the lining will show around the top as a decorative band.

11. Knot the cord in several places, and sew the ends of it to the purse at either side seam to form a strap.

DESIGNER: Lynn B. Krucke

Polymer Pins

Stamp the surface of a sheet of polymer clay with images, trim around them with a blade, and mount them on a clay backing to make unusual, eye-catching pins.

YOU WILL NEED

Blocks of polymer clay in colors of your choice for pin

Block of black polymer clay for pin's backing

Rolling pin or pasta machine

Rubber stamps of your choice
(see page 126 for a list of the stamps we used)

Black permanent ink pad

Craft knife or tissue blade

Wax paper

Baking sheet

Polymer-friendly glaze or acrylic floor wax

Two-part epoxy glue

Pin back

Warning: Please follow general safety instructions for polymer clay. Kitchen tools that you use for clay (such as a pasta machine or rolling pin) should be dedicated for use with clay and not used again for preparing food. To protect surfaces, tape down wax paper, or work on a piece of ceramic tile or glass. Ventilate the room well when you bake polymer clay.

INSTRUCTIONS

1. Condition the clays before using them by kneading and rolling them in your hands to warm and soften them.

2. Use the rolling pin or pasta machine to roll out a sheet of conditioned clay for the face of the pin that is approximately 1/16 inch (1.6 mm) thick. Blend together two colors if you wish. Roll out a sheet of black clay of the same thickness and set it aside.

3. Ink a rubber stamp of your choice with black permanent ink, and carefully place the stamp onto the sheet of prepared clay. Press gently but firmly to transfer the image to the clay. Carefully remove the stamp from the clay to avoid distorting the image. Layer other stamp images on top, if you like.

4. Cut out the image with the craft knife or tissue blade.

5. Gently pick up the stamped clay piece, and place it on the sheet of black clay. Place a small piece of wax paper over the image, and press gently to adhere the two pieces of clay together. The wax paper will keep fingerprints off of the clay and prevent smearing.

6. Trim away the black clay with the knife or blade, following the shape of the image and leaving a narrow border/frame around the piece.

7. Bake the completed piece on a baking sheet according to manufacturer's instructions. Apply polymer-friendly glaze or acrylic floor wax to the baked and cooled piece. Affix the pin back with two-part epoxy glue.

Shoulder Bag

Print a random pattern with recycled or purchased stamps on fabric before cutting and assembling the fabric into a roomy bag.

DESIGNER: Camille Gibson

YOU WILL NEED

½ yard (45.7 cm) medium to heavyweight fabric such as cotton, broadcloth, or linen

Iron

Fabric scissors

½ yard (45.7 cm) of lining fabric

⅛ yard (11.4 cm) of fusible interfacing

Old newspapers or newsprint

Paintbrushes

Acrylic fabric paints in colors of your choice

Stamps made from recycled items
(see page 101 for instructions) or broad-based foam stamps in a couple of contrasting sizes

Wedge-shaped foam applicator brush

Old toothbrush

Straight pins

Sewing thread

Sewing machine

1¾ yard (1.6 m) of decorative piping

2½ yards (2.3 m) of 1-inch-wide (2.5 cm) trim

Sewing needle

Large metal snap for closure

Large decorative button

INSTRUCTIONS

1. Prewash the medium to heavyweight fabric before drying and pressing it. Cut out the following pieces from the fabric: two pieces that measure 12 x 15 inches (30.5 x 38.1 cm) each; base piece that measures 4 x 8½ inches (10.2 x 21.6 cm); and flap that measures 3½ x 6½ inches (8.9 x 16.5 cm).

2. Cut pieces of the same size from the lining fabric. Use the scissors to round the corners of the base pieces that you cut from both the fabric and the lining. Round one of the long sides of the flap and the flap lining. Set aside the lining pieces.

3. Cut out a piece of fusible interfacing identical to the flap. Following the manufacturer's instructions, fuse it to the wrong side of the flap.

4. Cover your work surface in old newspapers or newsprint.

5. Use the paintbrushes and acrylic fabric paints to paint swirls, squiggles, or other freehand designs onto your fabric.

6. Allow the paint to dry for 24 hours, and heat set it according to the manufacturer's instructions.

7. Next you'll use stamps of your choice to apply another layer of designs to the fabric. Choose the larger of the stamps to apply first. Apply the paint with a foam brush, and try stamping on some scrap pieces of fabric to determine the consistency that you need in order to get a clean image. Randomly stamp designs onto your fabric. Heat set the paint according to the manufacturer's instructions.

8. Fill in and overlap the previously painted images with the prints from the smaller stamps. Heat set the paint accordingly.

9. Clean the stamps gently under lukewarm running water with an old toothbrush. Allow them to air-dry.

10. With the right sizes of the fabric together, pin the long side edges of the two sides of the bag together. Machine-

stitch the seam with a ⅝-inch (1.6 cm) seam allowance.

11. Pin and stitch pieces of the decorative piping to the upper edge of the bag, to the curved edge of the flap, and the base piece.

12. Pin the base to the sides of the bag, and stitch twice for strength. Trim seam allowance.

13. Cut the trim for the strap in half, and pin the pieces together with the wrong sides facing each other. Stitch together both pieces around the edges to create a reinforced strap.

14. Place each end of the strap inside the bag at the side seams, 1 inch (2.5 cm) down from the top. Machine-stitch the straps into place, making an X in a box for strength.

15. With a ⅝-inch (1.6 cm) seam allowance, stitch the side seams of the lining together, and stitch the bag lining base piece to the bottom.

16. With the right sides together, stitch the flap lining and flap together. Trim the seam allowance to ¼ inch (6 mm), and clip the curves.

17. Turn the flap right side out, and press it. Center the flap at the top of the bag, and stitch a ⅝-inch (1.6 cm) seam allowance.

18. Press the upper edge of the purse lining down ½ inch (1.3 cm) to the wrong side of the lining. Place the lining in the bag. Machine topstitch close to the folded edge, or hand-stitch it into place.

19. Sew the bottom half of the snap 3 inches (7.6 cm) down and centered from top of outside of bag. Position and sew the top half of the snap inside the flap. Sew the decorative button on the top side of the flap.

DESIGNER: Sandy Donabed

Classy Photo Pouch

Use the same stamping materials that were used for the project on pages 56 to 57 to make this pouch that can be used to hold photos or carried as a hand purse.

YOU WILL NEED

Fabric scissors

Uncolored cotton duck
or other durable fabric cut into piece that
measures 6 x 15 inches (15.2. x 38. 1 cm)

Dark lining fabric cut into piece that measures
6 x 15 inches (15.2 x 38.1 cm)

Children's shoes with bold,
treaded soles (use shoes that
you don't mind getting paint on,
such as those from a thrift store or ones
that your children have outgrown)

Alphabet-shaped stamps

Fabric paints of your choice
(we used black, brown, white,
bronze, copper, and silver)

Disposable polystyrene food trays,
egg carton, or other palette

Large sewing needle

Linen twine or jute

Iron

Sewing machine

Old credit card

INSTRUCTIONS

1. Use scissors to round off the last 3 inches (7.6 cm) of the length of each piece of fabric to form a flap.

2. Use the process described in the project on pages 99 to 101 to stamp the uncolored fabric piece with shoe prints and alphabet stamps.

3. After the fabric paint is completely dry, thread the large needle with twine or jute, and sew decorative French knots randomly on the flap of the piece, leaving room for attaching a tassel in the center later.

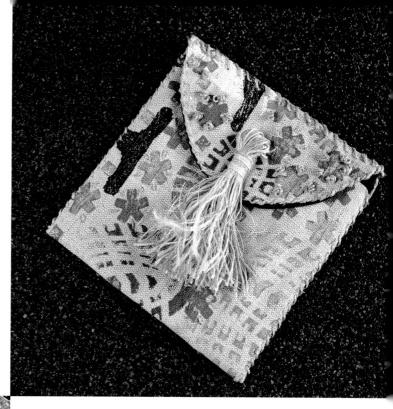

4. With the right sides together, pin the lining and the stamped fabric piece together. Sew a ½-inch (1.3 cm) seam around the edges, leaving a 3-inch (7.6 cm) opening on one side for turning the fabric. Clip the corners.

5. Turn the piece so that the stamped fabric is on the outside. Press the piece so that all the seams are flat, and press in the edges of the open seam. Fold the bottom part of the purse up where indicated on the pattern, and pin it into place at the side seams.

6. Thread the large needle with twine or jute, and whipstitch the sides of the purse together, moving from the bottom of the bag to the top. Ties off the ends of the thread on the inside of the bag.

7. Whipstitch the border of the flap with twine or jute.

8. Wrap twine or jute around the length of an old credit card until you have about a 1-inch (2.5 cm) wide band of twine. Cut the twine on one end, and remove it in a bundle.

9. Wrap the bundle with more twine about an inch (2.5 cm) from the fold at the top. Tie off the wrap at the back.

10. Sew the tassel to the center of the purse flap, as shown.

DESIGNER: Lynn B. Krucke

Matchbox Amulet Pendant

Transform a humble matchbox into an elegant piece of wearable art with stamped polymer clay and the embellishment of beads.

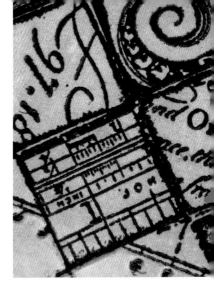

YOU WILL NEED

Small, empty matchbox

Glue brush

White glue

2 ounces (56 g) of white polymer clay

Rolling pin or pasta machine

Wax paper

Craft knife or tissue blade

Rubber stamp of your choice (see page 126 for information on the stamp we used)

Black permanent ink pad

Awl or ice pick

Baking sheet

Polymer-friendly glaze or acrylic floor wax

Small paintbrush

Burnt umber acrylic paint

Wire cutters

2 feet (61 cm) of 22-gauge black craft wire

A variety of small decorative beads (we used around 30 beads)

Wooden food skewer or narrow wooden dowel

Soft cotton rag

Tweezers

Scissors

3 yards (2.7 m) of satin cord or waxed linen in color that complements beads

Thin metal nail file (optional)

INSTRUCTIONS

1. Pull out and set aside the drawer of the matchbox. Use the paintbrush to coat the outside of the box (not the drawer) with a thin layer of white glue. Set the box aside to dry. (The glue provides a "key" for the polymer clay, result ing in a strong bond between the polymer clay and the paper box once it is baked.)

2. Condition the white clay by kneading and rolling it in your hands to warm and soften it. Place a piece of wax paper on your work surface. Use the rolling pin or pasta machine to roll out a sheet of conditioned clay approximately $\frac{1}{16}$ inch (1.6 mm) thick.

3. Trim the sheet of clay with the craft knife or tissue blade to 4 x 2$\frac{1}{4}$ inches (10.2 x 5.7 cm), and remove the excess. Save the scraps for later.

4. Ink the rubber stamp with black permanent ink, and carefully place the stamp onto the sheet of prepared clay. Press gently but firmly to transfer the image to the clay. Remove the stamp from the clay carefully to avoid distorting the stamped image. Repeat the image to fill the sheet, if needed, and don't worry about the image bleeding off the edge of the clay.

5. Place the drawer of the matchbox back inside it. Flip the clay over so that the stamped face of it is on the wax paper. Place one edge of the matchbox on top of the clay at one end, and begin wrapping the clay around the box. Keep the wax paper between the clay and your fingers to prevent smears and fingerprints. Work carefully to ensure that no air is trapped between the clay and the box.

6. Overlap the edges of the clay, and use the craft knife or tissue blade to cut through both layers of clay. Remove the excess clay, and smooth the seam with your fingers. Use the knife or blade to trim the excess clay from the top and bottom of the box.

7. From the scrap of clay, cut out a small rectangle to fit the bottom of the box. Apply it, and smooth out the seams with your fingers. Remove the drawer from the box, and set it aside.

8. Use an awl or ice pick to punch holes through the clay on the two narrow sides about $\frac{1}{2}$ inch (1.3 cm) from the top of the box. (Don't pierce the box.)

9. Place the box on the baking sheet, and bake according to the clay manufacturer's directions. After the box has cooled, seal it with a coat of polymer-friendly glaze or acrylic floor wax.

10. While the box is baking, paint the drawer with burnt umber acrylic paint. Use a fairly dry brush so that the drawer doesn't become too wet. If it swells, it won't fit well in the box. Allow the paint to dry.

11. Use the awl or ice pick to punch a hole in the middle of the front of the drawer to insert a drawer pull. Use the wire cutters to cut off about 1$\frac{1}{2}$ inches (3.8 cm) of black craft wire. Thread a small bead onto the wire until it reaches the center, bend the wire in half, and then twist the wire below the bead to hold it in place. From the inside of the drawer, insert the ends of the wire to the outside, and pull the wire out so that the bead catches on the inside. On the outside, thread a couple of small beads onto the doubled wire. Curl the ends of the wire around the skewer or dowel. Slide out the skewer or dowel, and make sure that the beads are secured by the wire when you pull on them. You now have a pull for your drawer.

12. Once the baked box has cooled, give it an antique finish by smearing it with the burnt umber acrylic paint. Use the cotton rag to remove excess paint before it dries. If the paint dries too quickly, dampen the rag and wipe it more. Add more paint if you want a darker look.

13. Use the wire cutters to cut two pieces of craft wire, each 9 inches (22.9 cm) long. Wrap each wire around the skewer or dowel, leaving about $\frac{1}{2}$ inch (1.3 cm) of wire uncurled at each end. Remove the curled wires.

14. With the awl or ice pick, pierce through the holes in the sides of the polymer box. On each side, insert both ends of one coiled wire. Use the tweezers to grab and pull the ends of the wires tight, and then flatten the ends of the wire inside the box.

15. Cut the cord or waxed linen into three equal pieces. Bundle them together, and tie a knot in the middle to secure them and form two separate sections of cords. String various beads onto the lower third of the cords, knotting them on either side as you add them. Leave a couple of inches (5.1 cm) of cord unstrung (on both sides).

16. Thread the unstrung cords down through the top of the wire spirals on either side of the box. Add beads to the ends of the cords on the other side. When you're finished, the beads should catch on the spirals, and prevent the box from slipping off the cord.

17. Reinsert the drawer. If the drawer doesn't slide in smoothly, use a metal nail file to file away some of the upper edges of the matchbox.

Warning: Please follow general safety instructions for polymer clay. Kitchen tools that you use for clay (such as a pasta machine or rolling pin) should be dedicated for use with clay and not used again for preparing food. To protect surfaces, tape down wax paper, or work on a piece of ceramic tile or glass. Ventilate the room well when you bake polymer clay.

DESIGNER: Kinga Britschgi

Faux Wood Jewelry

This unusual necklace, pin, and earrings prove the amazing versatility of polymer clay and the never-ending possibilities of stamping.

YOU WILL NEED

1 ounce (28 g) of translucent polymer clay

1 ounce (28 g) of tan polymer clay

Rolling pin and pasta machine

Mat knife or cutting blade

Rubber stamps of your choice
(see page 126 for a list of the stamps we used)

Wooden skewer

Antiquing medium in light brown

Rags

Soft cloth for buffing

Pin back

Two-part epoxy glue

Jewelry or round-nose pliers

6 jump rings

2 earring wires

20-inch (50.8 cm) narrow leather cord

6 small metal beads or other beads of your choice

INSTRUCTIONS

1. Condition the clays before use by kneading and rolling each in your hands to warm and soften them. Roll out a thin sheet of each clay with the rolling pin or pasta machine. Stack the sheets, and cut them in half.

2. Restack the sheets, alternating the colors of the clay. Roll out the stack to create a grainy wood appearance.

3. Repeat the cutting, stacking, and rolling several times, and keep the grainy appearance. When the "grains" appear very fine, cut and stack them for the last time without rolling out the clay.

4. Cut the stacked polymer clay sheet into narrow strips and lay them next to one another with the grainy side up. Roll the surface gently so that the strips will bond together. Don't overdo it.

5. Cut out free-form shapes for the necklace, pin, and earrings, making use of the uneven edges of the sheet where the strips lend the piece an interesting and natural look. Smooth the edges of the pieces with your fingertips.

6. Stamp the pieces randomly, pressing the stamps gently into the clay to avoid shadow lines. Allow some of the stamped designs to run off the edges so that only por-

tions of the images are visible. Make small holes with the wooden skewer in the earrings and the pendant where the jump rings will go.

7. Make four beads to accompany the pendant by rolling small bits of the mixed clay into balls. Poke a skewer through them to create holes. Leave them on the skewer.

8. Place your stamps on a hard surface with the printed side up. Roll the skewer and beads against any of your stamps to impress them. Remove the beads from the skewer very carefully.

9. Bake all the polymer pieces according to the clay manufacturer's instructions. Allow them to cool.

Free-form shapes lend the impression of wood to this stamped polymer pin.

10. Rub antiquing medium onto the pieces, making sure that it gets into the stamped lines. Wipe off the excess with a rag. Repeat this process if you want the pieces to be darker. Buff them with a soft cloth.

11. Attach the pin back to the pin with two-part epoxy glue. Use the pliers to attach the jump rings and earring wires to each of the holes in the earrings. Attach two jump rings to the hole in the pendant.

Warning: Please follow general safety instructions for polymer clay. Kitchen tools that you use for clay (such as a pasta machine or rolling pin) should be dedicated for use with clay and not used again for preparing food. To protect surfaces, tape down wax paper, or work on a piece of ceramic tile or glass. Ventilate the room well when you bake polymer clay.

12. String your beads and the pendant onto the narrow leather cord. Add clay and other beads on either side of the pendant. Adjust the length as you like, and cut off the excess. Knot the ends together.

Painted & Stamped Vest

A painterly, spontaneous pattern created by bleaching, painting, and stamping enlivens this colorful vest. The stamps are made from recyled materi-als, proving that you need only a bit of imagination to create your own printable objects.

DESIGNER: Camille Gibson

YOU WILL NEED

100% cotton broadcloth or linen in dark color
(check pattern for amount)

Iron

Mild detergent

Old sheets or towels

Plastic trash bags

Rubber gloves

Bleach

Small glass container

Synthetic paintbrushes for painting your designs

Acrylic fabric paints in light colors

Stamps made of recycled materials
(see next page) or foam stamps with bold design

Acrylic fabric paint in gold or other metallic color

Rag or paper towels

Purchased vest pattern of your choice

Thread and notions
(as called for on pattern)

Straight pins

Fabric scissors

Sewing machine and thread

INSTRUCTIONS

1. Prewash and dry your fabric. Iron out any wrinkles.

2. Fill your kitchen or bathroom sink with water and mild detergent.

3. To protect your lungs from the bleach, open a window in the room that you plan to work in, or work on a table outside. Fold the sheets or towels to create padding on your work surface. Cover them with the plastic trash bags.

4. Lay your prewashed and dried fabric on top of the padded surface. Put on rubber gloves. Pour a small amount of bleach into the glass container. Dip the synthetic brush in bleach and start "painting" a freehand design on the fabric. Be spontaneous and splatter the bleach, taking care not to get any on your skin or in your eyes. (Bear in mind that you'll eventually be cutting this fabric into the garment shapes, and too big of a design may be lost on the finished vest.) Keep an eye on how the bleach is discharging the color.

5. When the bleach reaches an effect that you like, rinse the fabric in soapy water followed by clear water when you want to stop the process. (You can begin again later if you need to keep the discharged areas a desired color.) Work section by section in this manner, if necessary. After rinsing, hang the fabric to dry. Press out any wrinkles after it has dried.

6. Place the fabric on the padded work surface again. Paint on random designs with acrylic fabric paints that complement your discharged design. Again, be spontaneous and have fun. Rinse the brush if needed, but avoid working with too wet of a brush. You don't want to soak the fabric; instead, the strokes should go on fairly dry.

7. Allow the paint to dry for at least 24 hours, and follow the paint manufacturer's instructions for setting the paint.

8. Lay out the fabric again. Use your stamps to randomly stamp additional designs with a metallic-colored paint. While you do this, clean the stamp with rags or paper towels as needed. Allow the paint to dry and set.

9. Cut out the pieces of your vest from the pattern, and sew it together.

How to Make
Down-&-Dirty Stamps
FROM RECYCLED STUFF

Look no further than your own
kitchen, and you'll find materials
that you can make into simple
but elegant stamps.

Polystyrene food trays and metal jar lids
can be used to make simple stamps.

YOU WILL NEED

Scrap paper

Pencil

Scissors

Black, fine-tip marker

Polystyrene food trays or thin,
foam dishwashing sheets

Craft knife
(if using polystyrene food trays)

Hot glue gun

Metal jar lids

INSTRUCTIONS

1. Draw some simple, broad designs onto sheets of scrap
paper. Think about how they will translate into stamps
when you use them. Cut them out with the scissors.

2. Use the black marker to trace them onto the polystyrene
material or thin foam dishwashing sheets. Cut out the
designs with the craft knife (for polystyrene) or scissors (for
foam).

3. Carefully hot glue your stamp cutouts to the jar lids. Use
the lid as a handle for holding your stamp when you print it.

DESIGNER: Karen Timm

Flying Fish Umbrella

Whether it's leaping lizards or flying fish that you choose to print, your stamped umbrella is sure to make a splash.

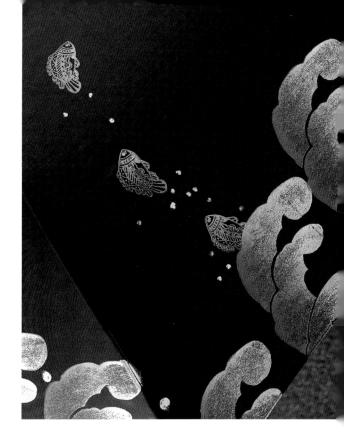

YOU WILL NEED

Black umbrella

Clothes steamer (optional)

Photocopy of wave template
(see page 125)

#2 Pencil

Masking tape

4 x 6-inch (10.2 x 15.2 cm) rubber sheet
made for carving
(available at art supply stores and craft stores)

Set of linoleum cutting tools

Newspapers or newsprint

Scrap of black nylon fabric

Tubes of oil-based printing inks in blue,
yellow, magenta, and white
(available at an art supply store)

Palette knife

Inking palette such as a sheet of glass
that measures at least 12 inches (30.5 cm) square

2 hard rubber brayers
(made for printmaking, available at art supply stores): one
2½ inches (6.4 cm) wide and one 4 inches
(10.2 cm) wide

Fish stamp
(see page 126 for the stamp that we used)

Book (or any hard surface) that measures about
5 x 7 inches (12.7 x 17.8 cm)

Vegetable oil made for cooking

Paper towels

Straight pin with plastic ball head

INSTRUCTIONS

1. Open the umbrella, and steam out the wrinkles, if needed.

2. Rub a #2 pencil back and forth on the back of the photocopied wave template until you've covered all areas that relate to the image on the front. Turn the template over, and tape it close to the top edge of the rubber sheet. Use the pencil to trace the lines of the wave on the front (they will transfer to the sheet when you do this).

3. Use the set of linoleum carving tools to carve the block (see pages 11 and 12 for more information). Keep in mind that you'll be cutting away the parts that will NOT be printed, so take care to remove only those parts. Take your time as you do this, and always cut away from your hands. If you make a major mistake, turn the block over and start again.

4. Cover your work surface with newspapers or newsprint. Place the scrap fabric, oil printing inks, palette knife, inking palette, and smaller brayer on your work surface. Squeeze out a small amount of white, yellow, and magenta printing ink onto the inking palette. Use the palette knife to mix up various bits of color to produce oranges and pinks. Leave these spots of color on the palette (not thoroughly mixing the colors will produce the most interesting effects when you print!), and use the smaller brayer to roll out the ink. Cover the brayer with ink, and roll an even coat of it onto the small fish stamp.

5. To print the stamp, tear a piece of newspaper or newsprint large enough to cover the top of your book, and place the covered book inside the umbrella behind the area that you want to print (use the finished piece as a guide for placement of the fish images). Press the stamp evenly onto the umbrella's surface with good pressure.

104

One hand-carved stamp and one readymade stamp are used together to create a beautiful object.

Continue inking the stamp with the brayer, and create a pattern of arcs around the edge of the umbrella. Keep all of your printing between the seam lines. Place the umbrella in a safe place to dry.

6. Clean up the inks with cooking oil and paper towels. Roll the brayer on a paper towel to remove the ink and then rub it with a bit of oil to remove any leftover ink.

7. At the top of your ink palette, squeeze out 1 inch (2.5 cm) or so (left to right) of white, blue, and magenta. Mix together some of the blue and magenta to create a violet. Roll the 4-inch (10.2 cm) brayer over the inks from left to right, combining the palette of white, blue, and violet. With your wave stamp facing upright (waves pointing to the left), ink the block with the brayer.

8. Practice stamping on your scrap fabric until you like the results.

9. Tape a swatch of newspaper or newsprint on the outside of the umbrella along the seam line to the right of the section you plan to print first. Ink up the wave stamp.

10. Cover your book with a scrap of newspaper. Begin printing on the left side of each section. Hold the book under the umbrella for support, and press your block firmly against it. Press the stamp all over with your fingertips to make sure that all the ink transfers. Repeat the wave motif, and vary its height. Keep moving the swatch of newspaper to the right of the next section to be printed.

11. Dip the pinhead in the ink, and dab on small dots around the fish that look like water droplets. Clean up the palette and brayer with vegetable oil and paper towels. Allow the umbrella to dry for a day before using it.

DESIGNER: Nan Roche

Mokumé Gane Pin

Polymer clay and rubber stamps make a perfect marriage. This project uses the impression of both a positive rubber stamp and its negative. (Double-sided stamps are now available on the market that consist of both the positive and negative prints of one stamp.) This project also adapts an ancient Japanese metalworking technique—mokumé gane—for use on polymer clay.

YOU WILL NEED

1 ounce (28 g) each of white and terra-cotta brown polymer clay

2 ounces (56 g) of black polymer clay

Pasta machine

Brayer

Thin tissue blade made for use with polymer clay

Rubber stamp with positive and negative texture (see page 126 for the stamp that we used)

Cornstarch

Coarse sandpaper

Piece of wax paper or tissue paper

Burnishing tool such as a large spoon

Metal pin back

Piece of cardboard or parchment

Patina (consists of a metal-laden paint [copper, bronze, or iron] and a patina [copper sulfate] that oxidizes the paint)

Stiff brush

Paper towels

Vinyl gloves

Heat gun (optional)

400-grit and 600-grit wet/dry sandpaper for finishing piece

Piece of soft denim cloth

INSTRUCTIONS

1. Follow general safety measures for polymer clay as outlined on page 95. Condition 1 ounce (28 g) of black, white, and terra-cotta clay thoroughly (by hand or with the pasta machine). Set the pasta machine to the widest thickness, and roll the clay through it into a sheet that is as close to square as possible.

2. Layer the three sheets of clay in the following order: black, terra cotta, and white. Roll a brayer over the three layers to remove any air bubbles.

3. Pass this clay sandwich through the pasta machine, resulting in a tri-colored single sheet.

4. Cut the resulting sheet in half. Stack the two halves together, maintaining the color order, and roll them back through the pasta machine. You'll now have six layers of color. Repeat this process once more to generate 12 layers of color.

5. Cut off a square of laminated clay that is slightly larger than the size of your rubber stamp. Dust the piece with a bit of cornstarch to remove the natural stickiness of the clay. Press one of the sides (either the black or the white) of the layered clay sheet into either the positive or negative side of the stamp. Make sure that all of the depressions are filled with clay.

6. For a variation, repeat step 5, and press another piece of clay on the opposite side (black or white) with the positive or negative side of the stamp to give a different effect.

7. To reveal the clay layers, you'll use the thin tissue blade to carve through the top layer of your pieces before baking. To begin this process, lightly press the clay pieces (pressed side up) onto your work surface. Check to make certain that they won't move.

8. Hold the tissue blade in both hands between your thumb and forefingers, and bow the blade slightly. Draw the blade slowly across the uppermost surface of your pressed clay, shaving off a very thin layer of clay. (This takes a little practice to keep your blade parallel to the clay surface.) As you cut through, you will see the other color layers underneath and the pattern will be highlighted. If you cut too deeply by mistake, back the blade out, press the cut back together, and begin again.

9. Roll out a sheet of black clay that is thinner than your pressed piece. Lightly dust it with cornstarch, and place the clay onto the sandpaper. Place a piece of wax or tissue paper over the top. Use a broad, smooth tool such as the back of a wide spoon to burnish the clay into the sandpaper. Press hard to get the best texture. Peel the clay away from the sandpaper, and lay the textured side of it down on a piece of wax or tissue paper.

This double-sided stamp shows a positive texture (see page 126 for stamp credit).

10. Place the pressed piece faceup on the sheet of black clay, and lightly press the two together under wax or tissue paper.

11. Trim around the edges of the shape that you stamped with the tissue blade. (You can flex the blade to conform to a rounded shape, if needed.)

12. Slice a thin strip of black, textured clay, and add it to the front of the pin as embellishment.

13. When finished, turn the pin over, and position the pin back on the clay. Attach it with a small strip of black clay. Smooth the edges of the strip with your fingertip.

14. Lay the piece facedown on cardboard or parchment, and bake it according to the clay manufacturer's instructions.

15. As a further option, you can antique the surface of your pin with patinas. Apply the patina of your choice with a stiff brush that will push the paint into the cracks and depressions of the pin's surface. Use a folded piece of paper towel to wipe away the paint from the surface only, leaving paint in the depressions.

16. Put on the vinyl gloves. With the paint still damp, flood the surface with the patina. Avoid getting the patina on your skin. Allow the piece to dry slowly on your work surface, dry in the sun, or with the help of a heat gun. The oxidized colors will develop fully over time and deepen.

17. For a final finish, sand your pin with 400-grit followed by 600-grit wet/dry sandpaper. Dip it in water to keep the surface cool during sanding. After sanding, buff your pin with a piece of soft denim.

Rolled Polymer Bracelets

Use the delicate leftover shavings from a mokumé gane project to make these beautiful bracelets. Each bracelet has a different design revealed during the process of making it.

DESIGNER: Barbara McGuire

YOU WILL NEED

Piece of plain paper

Scissors

Tape

Ruler

1 ounce (28 g) of dark polymer clay

Leftover shavings from mokumé gane project
(see pages 106 to 108)

Tissue blade

INSTRUCTIONS

1. Cut a narrow strip of paper at least 8 inches (20.3 cm) long. Place it around your wrist, and tape it at the ends to hold it where it fits you comfortably, and you can take it on and off.

2. After you've determined the size of your bracelet by this process, untape the paper, and measure the length of it with the ruler. Make a note of this length.

3. Condition the dark clay, and roll it out into a long snake that is about ¾ inch (9.5 mm) in diameter and the length of your paper bracelet.

4. Place leftover scraps from the mokumé gane process beside the bracelet. (Shave off new layers from the scraps of laminated clay, if needed.)

5. Position these delicate scraps on the surface of your clay snake, and roll it back and forth to adhere them. Keep adding scraps and rolling until you like the look of the surface.

6. Connect the two ends of the snake to form a circle. Stand the bracelet up so that these ends are on your work surface, and gently roll the bracelet back and forth to join them.

7. Bake the clay according to the manufacturer's instructions.

The Gallery

On the following pages you'll find examples of work by fine artists that incorporate stamping in many different ways. Stamping is used as an integral part of a larger image that contains other media; or, in some cases, it dominates the composition.

Turn the page to see work by accomplished artists who work in mixed media, polymer clay, assemblage, fabric, paper, and more.

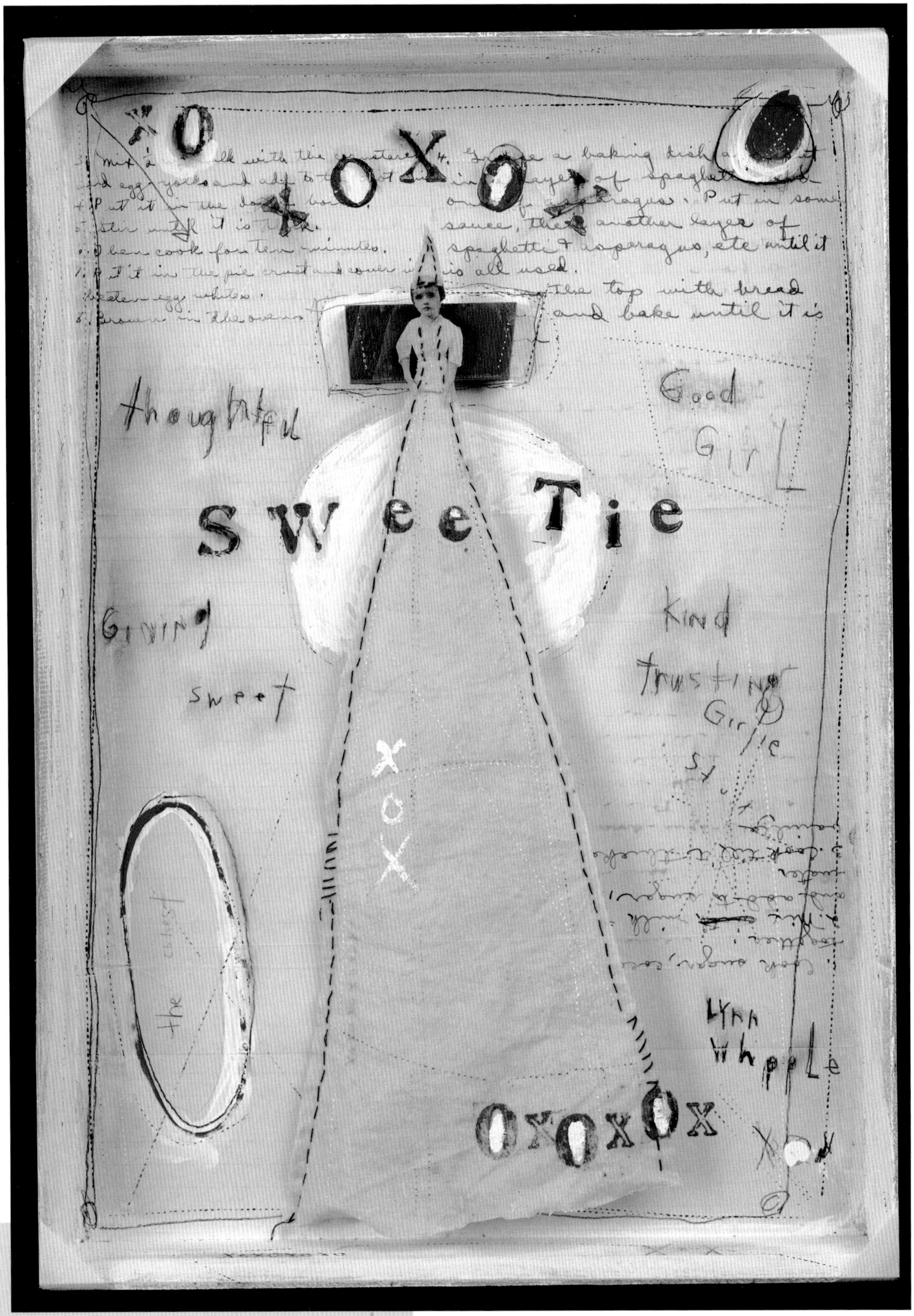

112

Lynne Whipple,
Sweetie, 2000,
Collage, fabric,
acrylic paint, found ledger pages, stamping with antique letter set,
14 x 10 x 1 in. (35.6 x 25.4 x 2.5 cm). Photo by Randall Smith

Janet Hofacker, **Untitled,** 1999,
Assemblage with stamped background, 8 x 5 ¾ x 3 in.
(20.3 x 14.6 x 7.6 cm)

113

Jeanne Williamson, **Textures, Maps
& Grids Series, #6**, 2000, Art quilt:
monoprinted, hand stamped with rubber
erasers and fabric paint on cotton fabric,
machine appliquéd and quilted,
51 x 35 in. (129.5 x 88.9 cm).
Photo by David Caras

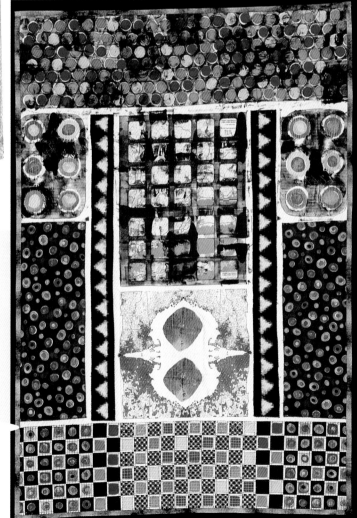

Elaine Plogman, *Ice Age*, 1999, Art quilt: cotton fabric
(some dyed, painted, or stamped using fabric paint),
machine pieced and quilted, 39 x 41 in. (99.1 x 104.2 cm)

Karen Page, **Untitled**, 2000, Painted and stamped cloth book,
Closed: 7 x 7 in. (17.8 x 17.8 cm)

Karen Page, **Untitled**,
2000, Handmade
portfolio, cover printed
with hand-carved stamp
made by the artist,
12 x 18 in.
(30.5 x 45.7 cm)

Nan Roche, **Glyph Vessel**, 1997, Stamped polymer clay vessel with a surface dusting of atomized metal powders, 4 x 3 in. (10.2 x 7.6 cm). Photo by artist

Nan Roche, **Animal Augrey 1 & 2**, 1998, Stamped on polymer clay vessels, Left to right: 5½ x 2½ (14 x 6. 4 cm), 7½ x 1½ in. (19.1 x 3.8 cm). Photo by artist

Judith Plotner, *In My Mother's Closet II*, 1998, Art quilt: dye monoprinted and commercial fabric, photo transferred, stamped, machine pieced
and appliquéd, hand quilted, 31½ x 27 in. (80 x 68.6 cm)

Janet Hofacker,
Untitled, 1999,
Collage with
stamped portions,
8 x 5 ¾ x 3 in.
(20.3 x 14.6 x 7.6 cm)

Virginia A. Spiegel, **June 14: Bumblebee Love**, 2000, Art quilt: Includes fabric paint on white cotton printed with large block stamp carved by the artist, 29 x 29 in. (73.7 x 73.7 cm). Photo by Joe Edom

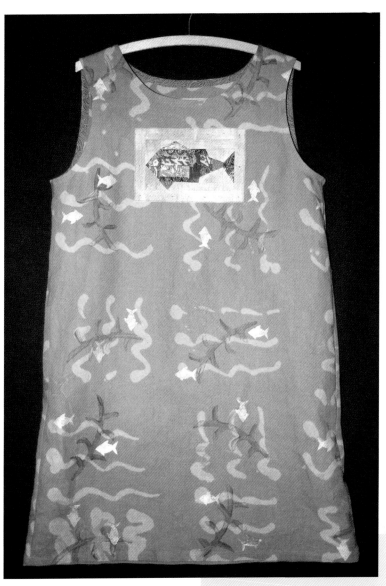

Camille B. Gibson, **The Lake Davis Fish**, 1998, Stamped and painted fabric using stamps made from recycled materials, Photo by artist

Barbara McGuire, **Dragonfly Book**, Inset panel of polymer clay and precious metal clay stamped with stamp designed by artist.

Elaine Plogman, **Hopscotch Heaven**, 1998, Art quilt: fabrics stamped with hand-carved blocks and fabric paint, machine pieced and quilted, 65 x 65 in. (1.6 x 1.6 m)

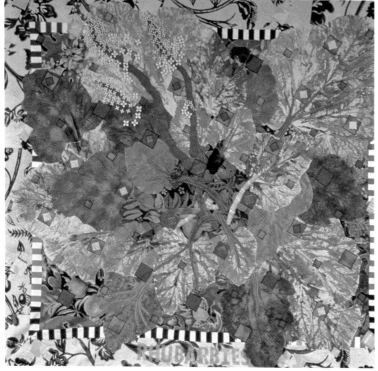

Sandra T. Donabed, **Rhubarbies**, 2000, Fabric collage made from leaf-stamped materials, 58 x 51 in. (147.3 x 129.5 cm)

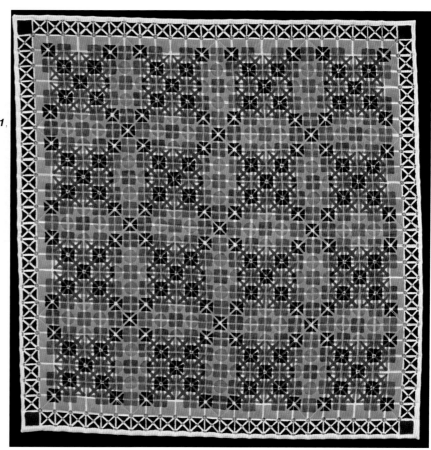

Jeanne Williamson, *4 x 4 Number 1*,
1991, Art quilt: hand stamped with
rubber erasers using fabric paint
on cotton, machine quilted,
30 x 30 in. (76.2 x 76.2 cm).
Photo by David Caras

Elaine Plogman, *We Are One*,
1997, Art quilt: block print on
cotton fabric with fabric paint,
machine pieced and quilted,
40 x 40 in. (101.6 x 101.6 cm)

Judith Plotner, *In My Mother's Closet*, 1998, Art quilt: dye monoprinted and commercial
fabric, photo transferred, stamped, machine pieced and appliquéd, hand quilted,
31¾ x 25¼ in. (80.6 cm x 64.1 cm)

Delda Skinner, *Primary Speech III*, 2000, Mixed media collage with stamping, 22 x 30 in. (55.9 x 76.2 cm)

Templates

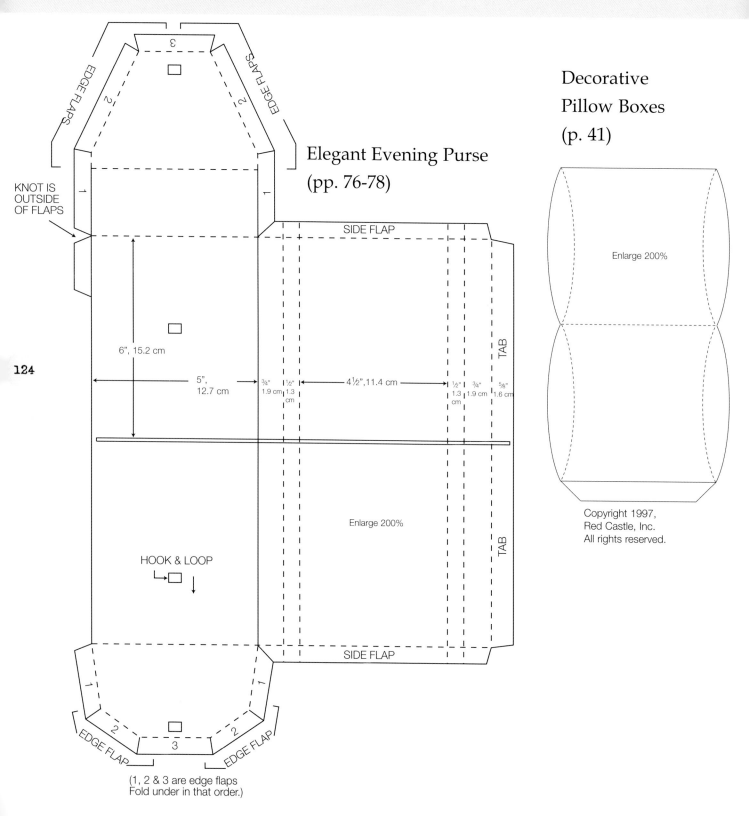

Elegant Evening Purse
(pp. 76-78)

EDGE FLAPS

3

2

2

EDGE FLAPS

KNOT IS
OUTSIDE
OF FLAPS

1

1

6", 15.2 cm

SIDE FLAP

TAB

5",
12.7 cm

¾"
1.9 cm

½"
1.3
cm

4½",11.4 cm

½"
1.3
cm

¾"
1.9 cm

⅝"
1.6 cm

Enlarge 200%

TAB

HOOK & LOOP

1

1

SIDE FLAP

EDGE FLAP

2

2

EDGE FLAP

3

(1, 2 & 3 are edge flaps
Fold under in that order.)

124

Decorative Pillow Boxes (p. 41)

Enlarge 200%

Swank Velvet Hat (pp. 79-81)

Flying Fish Umbrella (pp. 102-105)

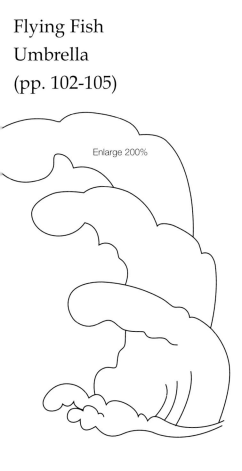

Enlarge 200%

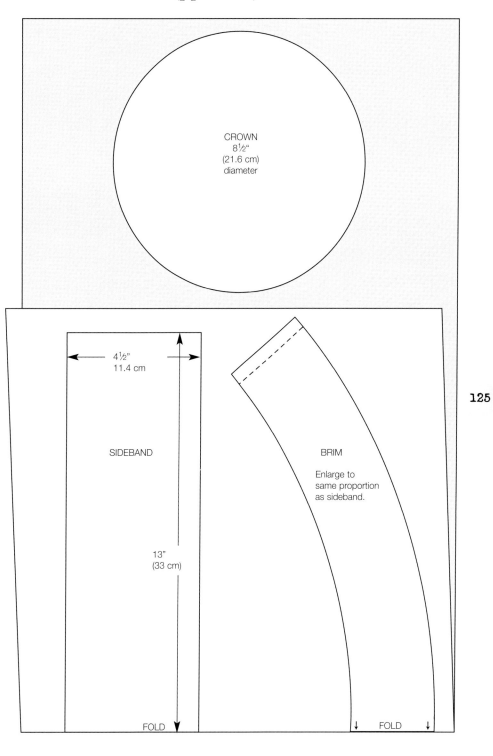

CROWN
8½"
(21.6 cm)
diameter

4½"
11.4 cm

SIDEBAND

13"
(33 cm)

FOLD

BRIM

Enlarge to
same proportion
as sideband.

FOLD   FOLD

Stamp and Supply Credits

After each project, the name of the company is listed, followed by a description of the stamp or the actual title of the stamp given to it by the company. The contact information for the companies appears on the following page.

Turtle stamp (page 21), Design Innovations/Creative Claystamps, stamp designed by Cynthia Toops

EmbossedNotebooks/Kauffman (p. 27), Red Castle, Inc., "Tactile Impressions I & II" sheets (pattern stamps [#49010 and 49020])

Mona Lisa Altar/Anderson (pp. 28-31), Sunday International (alphabet stamps)

Stamped Mail Art/Udell (pp. 36-38), Imprints (fossil stamp [detail on p. 38]), Ed Kinsey (deer and bison stamps), Zettiology (petroglyph stamp)

Accordion Book/Krucke (pp. 39-40), Magenta (dragonfly stamps)

Decorative Pillow Boxes/Kauffman (p. 41), Red Castle, Inc., "Tactile Impressions" (all stamps), Red Castle, Inc., "Fit It" (box templates)

CollagedScrapbook/Taormina (pp. 42-43), Rubber Stampede (border stamp)

Stamped Gift Ensemble/Kauffman (pp. 44-45), Red Castle (Gibson girls, tiny heart-shaped seed [from "Flying Seeds" sheet] and "Tactile Impressions I" [for backgrounds]), Sulyn Industries (die-cut lantern boxes)

Tag Art/Luperini (pps. 46-47), Stampin' Up ("Petite Patterns," "Bold Hearts and Flowers," "Fantastic Foliage," "Beautiful Butterflies," "PSX" [numbers]); Colorbox ("Amber Cat's Eye," "Terra Cotta Cat's Eye"); Acey Deucy, ("Summer"); A Stamp in the Hand ("Script")

Hanging Book/Britschgi (pp. 50-51), Appaloosa Art Stamps (dragon), Above the Mark (Chinese-English dictionary page)

Masked Magnets/Britschgi (pp. 52-53), Ornamentum (Roman numbers), Non Sequitur, "Greco-Roman Collage Elements" plate (all other stamps)

Overprinted Pillow/Taormina (pp. 60-61), Rubber Stampede (leaf and fossil)

Plush Botanic Cushions/Lee (pp. 62-65) Rubber Stampede ("Rose Leaf" [A2491E], "Aspen" [A2496F], "Eucalyptus" [A2493F], "Bamboo Weave" [A2245C], "Fancy Leaf Flourish"

[A2254E]), Leather Factory (leather supplies)

CD Clock: Time for Art/Krucke (pp. 66-68), Stampin' Up (numbers), Stamper's Anonymous (crackle stamp), Junque (all other stamps)

Classical Art Calendar/Britschgi (pp. 69-70), Stamper's Anonymous ("Art" text background), Ornamentum ("Herba" text), Rubber Stampede (distressed alphabet stamps), Non Sequitur, "Greco-Roman Collage Elements" plate (all other stamps)

Goddess Clock/Britschgi (pp. 71-72), Appaloosa Art Stamps ("Book of Death"), Non Sequitur, "Egyptian Collage Elements" plate (all other stamps)

Celtic Table Topper/Damelio (pp. 73-75), Rubber Stampede (Celtic knot)

Elegant Evening Purse/Timm (pp. 77-78), Magenta (design stamp)

Swank Velvet Hat/Timm (pp. 79-81) Hero Arts (Quatro Elements Ornamental Leaves)

Airy Scarf/Kauffman (p. 83), Magenta, ERA Graphics, and Rubber Stamps of America (feathers); Red Castle, Inc., ("Flying Seed")

Polymer Pins/Krucke (pp. 86-87), Stamper's Anonymous (pear), Junque (woman and letters), Judikins (fan), Acey Deucy (stamps used on silver and green pins)

Matchbox Amulet Pendant /Krucke (pp. 92-95), Stamper's Anonymous (design stamp)

Faux Wood Jewelry/Britschgi (pp. 96-98), Ornamentum ("Herba" stamp), Rubber Stampede (leaves and Tuscan elements)

Flying Fish Umbrella/Timm (pp. 103-105), JudiKins ("Sea Life" [#6568H])

Mokumé Gane Pin/Roche (pp. 106-108), Design Innovations/Creative Claystamps, stamp designed by Nan Roche (Chinese script)

Company Credits

Stamps and other products used by the designers in this book were produced by one of the following companies. We suggest that you first browse the website of the company to find the stamp that you want. You can order stamps directly from many of the companies—other companies will give you a list of retailers so that you can visit the store nearest to you. Some companies will send you a catalogue of their stamps to browse.

Companies that are noted on their sites as "angel" companies usually allow you to use their images on a limited number of hand-stamped items to sell without worrying about copyright. (They do ask that you not mechanically, digitally, or otherwise reproduce the images after you stamp them.) Always read each company's copyright statement in their catalog or on their website. If you plan to sell items stamped with images from a non-angel company, contact the company for clarification of their copyright policy and proper authorization. When in doubt, always consult the company or a copyright attorney.

Another resource for finding rubber stamps is www.rubberstamps.com. Go to this rubber stamp directory, and you can search for rubber stamp stores near you as well as companies.

Above The Mark
P.O. Box 8307
Woodland, California 95776
Phone: (530)666-6648
www.abovethemark.com
info@abovethemark.com

Acey Deucey
P.O. Box 194
Ancram, New York 12502
Phone: (518)398-5108
Fax: (518)398-6364

Appaloosa Art Stamps
P.O. Box 85
Viola, Idaho 83872
Phone: (866)882-0333
www.aasimagick.com

A Stamp In The Hand, Co.
20507 S. Belshaw Avenue
Caron, California 90746
Phone: (310)884-9700
Fax: (310)884-9888
www.astampinthehand.com

Colorbox
Clearsnap, Inc.
Box 98
Anacortes, Washington 98221
Phone: (800)448.4862
Fax: (360)293.6699
www.clearsnap.com
contact@clearsnap.com

Design Innovations/Creative
Claystamps
P.O. Box 472334
San Francisco, California 94147
Phone/fax: (415)922-6366

ERA Graphics
2476 Ottawa Way
San Jose, California 95130
Tel: (408)364-1124
Fax: (408)364-1126
www.eragraphics.com

Fit It
(see Red Castle, Inc.)

Hero Arts
1343 Powell Street
Emeryville, California 94608
Phone: (800)822-4376
Fax: (800)441-3632
(stamps made for retailers)

Imprints
P.O. Box 938
Forest Hill, California 95631
www.graphistamp.com

Judikins
17832 S Harvard Boulevard
Gardena, California 90248
Phone: (310)323-6619
Fax: (310)515-1115
www.judi-kins.com

Junque
P.O. Box 466
Mansfield Center, Connecticut
06250-0466
www.junque_art.homestead.com
junquegrrl@hotmail.com

The Leather Factory
3847 E. Loop 820 South
Fort Worth, Texas 76119
(877)532-8437

Magenta Art Stamps
2275 Bombardier
Sainte Julie Quebec
J3E2J9 Canada
Phone: (450)446-5253
Fax: (450)464-6353
www.magentarubberstamps.com
info@magentarubberstamps.com

Non Sequitur
P.O. Box 5836
Pasadena, California 77508-5836
Fax: (713)475-9506
www.nonsequiturstamps.com
nonsequitur@nonsequiturstamps.com

Ornamentum
20611 E. Bothell Everett Hwy.
Bothell, Washington 98012
Phone: (425)481-6509
www.cdad.com/orn

Red Castle, Inc.
P.O. Box 39-8001
Edina, Minnesota 55439-8001
www.red-castle.com

Rubber Stampede, Inc.
2550 Pellissier Place
Whittier, California 90601-1505
Phone: (562)695-7969
Fax: (562)695-4227
www.rubberstampede.com

Rubber Stamps of America
P.O. Box 567
Saxtons River, Vermont 05154
Phone: (800)553-5031
www.stampusa.com

Stamper's Anonymous
The Creative Block
20613 Center Ridge Road
Rocky River, Ohio 44116
Phone: (888)326-0012
Fax: (888)333-7992
www.stampersanonymous.com

Stampin' Up
Phone: (800)782-6787
www.stampinup.com

Sulyn Industries
11927 West Sample Road
Coral Springs, Florida 33065
Phone: (954)755-2311

Sunday International
5672 Buckingham Dr.
Huntington Beach, California 92649
Phone: (800)401-8644
Fax: (714)901-2466
www.sundayint.com
info@sundayint.com

Zettiology Rubber Stamps & Mythos
39570 SE Park St. #201
Snoqualmie, Washington 98065
Phone: (425)888-3191
Fax: (425)888-8774
www.zettiology.com

Project Designers

Kathy Anderson (Kent, Washington) lives with her husband of 34 years, and enjoys passing her love of art on to her children. Her work has been published in magazines and books, and she is a member of the Society of Craft Designers.

Tana L. H. Boerger (Washington, D.C.) is an artist and entrepreneur who, after twenty years of buying and selling companies, returned to her true passion, the creation of art. Currently, she combines business and art by creating designs that are licensed to manufacturers of home decor items.

Kinga Britschgi (Boise, Idaho) was born and raised in Hungary where she earned a degree in Art Education. She has been living in the United States for five years. Her work focuses on collage and stamping and is widely published in magazines and books.

Lynn Damelio (Northern California) has been designing stamp projects for the six years and has been a contributing designer to several stamp books and magazines. She has appeared on several craft television programs and teaches workshops at major trade shows.

Sandy Donabed (Westwood, Massachusetts) has played with fabric all of her life but usually returns to art quilts. She employs all sorts of surface design techniques in her fabric work and says that she has "the world's largest collection of alphabet stamps."

Camille B. Gibson (Hillsborough, New Hampshire) holds a degree in Design Technology for Theatre and Film with an emphasis in Costume Design from the State University of New York College at Purchase. She has done extensive costuming for theatre, film, and television in New York City. Her work is now focused on quilting, soft sculpture, and clothing designs.

Justin Hawkins (New York, New York) is an elementary school teacher and illustrator. He works primarily with relief printmaking, and his illustrations have appeared in editorial and commercial publications. He lives in Brooklyn with his wife and daughter.

Maggie D. Jones (Greer, South Carolina) is a photographer who teaches high school art. In her spare time, she loves to dabble with design and experiment with unusual combinations of materials.

Judi Kauffman (Chevy Chase, Maryland) is a designer and writer whose interests range from rubber stamping to collage to needlepoint and weaving. She teaches the art of stamping and is a published author of books and magazine articles. She has designed a line of stamps for Red Castle Rubber Stamps.

Lynn B. Krucke (Summerville, South Carolina) is a mixed media artist whose interests include paper arts, beads, fiber, fabric, and polymer clay. In addition to her design work, Lynn teaches a variety of mixed-media classes at rubber stamp stores around the Southeast.

Kari Lee (Houston, Texas) has worked in the arts and crafts industry for nineteen years. Her most recent years as a designer in charge of research and development for The Leather Factory have opened the door to many creative possibilities for surfaces and embellishments. Kari lives with her husband, Johnny, and her children Tiffani and Trey.

Nicole Novak Luperini (Tarzana, California) is a collage and mixed media artist. She holds a degree in Biology and Studio Art from Hood College, and now works in interior design. She has a passion for fabric, pattern, color, and natural textures in her work.

Barbara McGuire (San Francisco, California) is the author of the recently published *Foundations in Polymer Clay Design*. In her role as Creative Director for Accent Import Export, she promotes and presents projects in polymer clay. She has appeared 10 times on the Carol Duval Show and has a monthly feature in the magazine Craftworks. Her position allows her to be at the forefront of new product development, and she is currently working on a line of stamps for clay.

Karen Page (Port Townsend, Washington) has had an interest in fiber art since her childhood when she knitted, embroidered, and made her own clothes. Since then she has pursued interests in weaving, basket making, quilting, beading, art to wear, paper, and book making. She has shared techniques through teaching in the United States and Canada.

Nan Roche (College Park, Maryland) is the author of the first comprehensive how-to book on polymer clay entitled *New Clay: Techniques And Approaches To Jewelry Making* (Flower Valley Press, Inc., 1992). She is currently working on her second book about polymer clay. She teaches, writes magazine articles, and appears on television shows to promote and teach about polymer clay. She is an active member of the National Polymer Clay Guild.

Grace Taormina (Northern California) has been designing projects and products for Rubber Stampede for over eight years. She is the author of *The Complete Guide to Rubber Stamping* and *The Complete Guide to Decorative Stamping* (Watson-Guptill). She teaches the art and craft of rubber stamping at major trade show events and is a regular guest at several craft television programs.

Karen Timm (Madison, Wisconsin) worked in advertising for ten years before she started her own business called "Books About You". She creates hundreds of one-of-a-kind handmade blank books. Her work is sold and in both America and Europe.

Luann Udell (Keene, New Hampshire) is a nationally-exhibited mixed media artist with a secret passion for carving her own stamps. Her fiber assemblages, embellished with her own handmade polymer clay artifacts, are inspired by the Ice Age cave paintings of Lascaux, France. She creates cards and framed prints with her carved images of horses, red stag, and bison such as those found painted on the walls of the 17,000 year old cave.

Emily Wilson Hintz (Smithville, Tennessee) is a fulltime sculptor who exhibits in the Southeastern United States. She holds a B.F.A. in painting from Memphis College of Arts in Tennessee.

Index